A Father in the Faith

A Father in the Faith
J. Elwyn Davies (1925-2007)

Edited by John Emyr

BRYNTIRION PRESS

©Bryntirion Press 2012

First published 2012

ISBN 978 1 85049 244 3

Scripture quotations are from the Authorised (King James) version

Evangelical Movement of Wales

The EMW works in both Welsh and English and seeks to help Christians and churches by:
* running children's camps and family conferences
* providing theological training and events for ministers
* running Christian bookshops and a conference centre
* publishing magazines and books

Bryntirion Press is a ministry of EMW

Past issues of EMW magazines and sermons preached at our conferences are available on our website: www.emw.org.uk

Published by Bryntirion Press, Bryntirion, Bridgend CF31 4DX, Wales, in association Evangelical Press, Faverdale North, Darlington, DL3 0PH, UK

Contents

A Father in the Faith

Extracts from the Preface to the Welsh Edition

'Remember them which have the rule over you, who have spoken unto
you the word of God: whose faith follow, considering
the end of their conversation.' (Hebrews 13:7)

'This shall be written for the generation to come: and the people
which shall be created shall praise the Lord.' (Psalm 102:18).

'Blessed are the dead which die in the Lord... that they may rest
from their labours; and their works do follow them.' (Revelation 14:13).

Why should we write of the late Rev. John Elwyn Davies (1925-2007) or
others of the servants of God who have gone to glory? Have they not
entered into their reward, and what purpose is there for us, now, to
speak of them? Is there not better work for us to take up, following their
example, rather than to be speaking of them? And has there not been
sufficient writing of tributes, which so easily slips into empty praising
and eulogising?

It is fitting that we should begin in this way, acknowledging the pitfalls.
However, we have the warrant of the Scriptures not to be satisfied with
mere silence. Indeed, we are commanded by the author of the Letter to
the Hebrews to remember those who ruled over us, especially those who
spoke the Word of God to us. The Psalmist also, looking into the future,
saw purpose in writing of the experiences and work of God's people, so
that 'the people which shall be created shall praise the Lord.'

This book is made up of glimpses of the life and work of Elwyn Davies
through the eyes of those who knew him. It it written as an expression

of gratitude for the service of one of God's servants in his generation. An open invitation was offered (in the pages of the *Cylchgrawn Efengylaidd* and in the Welsh Annual Conference of the Evangelical Movement of Wales) for anyone who wished to contribute to send their comments, and we thank all who responded to that offer. A typical example of the tributes received was that of Arfon Jones:

> 'One of the things that always struck me about the Rev. Elwyn Davies was his love of the Word. When listening to him preaching, speaking at a retreat, or leading a Bible study I was always amazed at his carefulness when handling the Scriptures. Every word was important. His respect for the Bible sprang from his love for his Saviour.
>
> He had the ability to share something of the excitement to be had when reading and meditating the Scriptures. He demonstrated the carefulness required when handling God's Word. As a young student in the 1970s, I always looked forward eagerly to hearing him preach. The gentleness of his character and strength of his convictions formed a powerful combination under God's hand.'

Some of the tributes appeared in the *Cylchgrawn Efengylaidd*, and I am grateful for the permission to reprint them here. Some had first appeared in the summer of 1990 when Elwyn Davies retired from his post of General Secretary of the Evangelical Movement of Wales. I am particularly grateful to Professor R. Geraint Gruffydd – who was a true friend to Elwyn Davies since their student days at Bangor – for his kind permission to include his valuable tribute.

As well as the tributes it was thought that an introduction, that would place Elwyn Davies in the Welsh context of his day and provide an appreciation of his vision and contribution, would be useful. I could not think of anyone more appropriate for this task than the Rev. Dr D. Eryl Davies. I am grateful to him for accepting the invitation. As a minister and pastor and as the past Principal of the Theological College of Wales, Bridgend, he had worked with Elwyn Davies for many years. And as a Christian author he has the ability of the historian and theologian to discern what is central and significant in the history.

Extracts from the Preface to the Welsh Edition

Together with the comments on Elwyn Davies I have also included some of his own writings. It is clearly a very short anthology. Its purpose, simply, is to provide a glimpse of some of the topics and meditations that took his attention. The first contribution, 'Amongst Berlin's Ruins', belongs to the period at the end of the Second World War and displays the sympathy of the author for his fellow-man in need. The article 'Remembering Celt' reveals the influence of that young Christian, before his untimely but victorious death, upon the life of Elwyn Davies and his contemporaries. 'Memories of Blaenau' refer to a very special period when the young people of Jerusalem Chapel, Blaenau Ffestiniog, experienced spiritual blessing, and became in their turn leaders in their various fields. The article 'Unwitting Backsliders' is an example of the instinct of a pastor administering a word in season – an importunate and anointed word which is as relevant today as when it first appeared. In 'God's Gift to a nation' we find Elwyn Davies's tribute to his friend and spiritual father, Dr D. Martyn Lloyd-Jones. 'The Secret of her Strength' is an example of a published sermon where the author presents an argument thoughtfully and effectively, leading the hearer and reader, step by step, to see and embrace the truth laid upon his heart. Finally, in the article 'Believe that ye receive' we have a meditation on the theme of the Christian teaching on prayer, with examples from the life of the author...

I am grateful to all who contributed to the volume. Thanks are due to Mair Eluned Davies – the 'helpmeet' for whom Elwyn Davies was so very thankful – for her interest in the book and her support. I am grateful to my wife, Gwen Emyr, for her invaluable help. Preparing the volume has been the means of our remembering a father and father-in-law who was so generous in his advice and support for us at all times.

John Emyr

Preface to the English Translation

'Porth yr Aur – Cofio J. Elwyn Davies',[1] edited by John Emyr, was published by Bryntirion Press in 2011. The Gold Gate of the title refers to one of the portals of Caernarfon Castle that reflects the sun's setting rays. Elwyn Davies would often mention it as he remembered his early years in Caernarfon. John Emyr chose the picture as a symbol of the central ministry and focus of the life of his father-in-law – that precious 'door' that opens into life to 'all who believe'.

Since its publication there have been many calls for the book to be translated into English. Some of the tributes first appeared in English in the pages of *The Evangelical Magazine of Wales*. These have been reproduced as first published, and we are again grateful to those authors who kindly consented for them to be reprinted here. The articles that were originally written in Welsh, some of them having first appeared in *Y Cylchgrawn Efengylaidd*, have been translated by John Aaron. The form of this English edition is exactly that of the original Welsh book except that a valuable tribute by the Rev. Alan Gibson describing Elwyn Davies's contribution to the work of the BEC (The British Evangelical Council) has been added.

.

Introduction

I would like to accomplish two things in this chapter, as a tribute to the Rev. J. Elwyn Davies. Firstly, I wish to share some personal memories and to express also my indebtedness to him and respect for him. Secondly, I am eager to discuss and expound a few principles which he considered very important. Without an understanding of these principles it is impossible to begin to appreciate either his work or the burden he felt for the gospel and for churches in Wales. But more of that later.

Memories

There are many memories of Elwyn I could share but I confine myself to the most important: memories I have of him when I was a student at Aberystwyth, then as a minister in Maesteg and Bangor, and also when I was Principal of the Evangelical Theological College of Wales (now renamed WEST) at Bryntirion, Bridgend. In each of these periods, Elwyn's support, fellowship and influence were crucial to me.

(a) I was a student at Aberystwyth for six years between 1953 and 1959, studying, firstly, theology, and then history and philosophy. I was converted there in February 1954 and as a result began attending both the Christian Union and the Theological Society that was affiliated to the Inter-Varsity Fellowship, now known as the Universities and Colleges Christian Fellowship (UCCF). I received considerable help in these meetings and good teaching in the Word. One of the regular speakers at the Aberystwyth Christian Union was Elwyn, and when he was appointed a member of the IVF staff in 1955 to care for the CUs of the Welsh University Colleges I began to know him better.

It is impossible to forget, for example, the series of messages he gave on the Lord's Prayer. Everyone felt the power that was in his ministry, and that emphasis on prayer was with him to the end of his life. I remember Elwyn also as the main speaker in a mission held in the University College in 1957/58. He spoke several times, explaining the gospel, but he was very worried about one particular central meeting which the University Vice-Principal was to chair. Elwyn was concerned that he might compromise the message of the gospel out of fear or of seeking to please such an important individual, and he asked us to pray particularly for the evening's ministry. And we received an abundant answer to our prayers.

Without perhaps his realising it at the time, Elwyn became a mentor to me, particularly during the two-year period when I led the Christian Union at the College. Some years later, Mair, his wife, said, 'Elwyn was always looking out for people who had the potential for leadership, and spent time with them… He believed that God called people to the work of the kingdom, but that there was always a need to discern these, to spend time with them and to support them continually.'[2]

One other memory stands out for me. At the end of my second term in 1958, Elwyn offered me transport from Aberystwyth to Bala so that I might stay overnight at Eryl Aran, the new Centre of the Evangelical Movement of Wales, and so that we might have times of prayer together for the work in the College. I agreed and it was a profitable experience of fellowship with Elwyn and Mair, and also with Gwilym and Beth Humphreys. The next day, Elwyn and I spent several hours together seeking the Lord for help in the student work in Aberystwyth, and this was the first time for me to have the experience of praying for an extended period, and to learn to pray on my knees. It was unforgettable and left a deep impression upon me.

On another occasion, the Christian Union arranged a mission in Barmouth during the College half-term in February, 1957. Some of the chapels welcomed the idea of holding preaching services and there would be opportunities for speaking at some local schools and for working with young people, together with some door-to-door visitation and tracting. Our great problem was that because of fear and lack of experience, only a very small number of students were willing to take part. When Elwyn heard this he advised us to pray further and he also arranged to come to us and speak on the Great Commission of the Lord Jesus (Matthew 28:18-20). We received a great challenge from his ministry that night. For example, having explained and applied the words, 'Lo, I am with you always, even to the end of the age', he asked us the question: 'If someone famous like Dr Martyn Lloyd-Jones, London, was to offer to come with you to Barmouth, would you be happy to go? And if you

Introduction

could go from door to door or speak in the schools with 'the Doctor' at your side, would you be happy to go?' We all smiled, and were greatly encouraged when he continued, 'But there is someone so very much more important and powerful than Lloyd-Jones who has promised to come – the Lord Jesus himself will be with you.' The result was that a considerable number from the Christian Union decided to be involved in the mission.

(b) Afterwards, when I was a minister at Maesteg (1959-1975) and at Bangor (1975-1985), I would see Elwyn often and he was a brother as well as a support to me in so many different ways. In conferences, committees, prayer meetings, preaching services and monthly fraternal meetings, I saw his burden for the gospel and for the churches, his concern also for revival and for the Welsh language work.

I was brought to realise at the end of one difficult but crucial meeting at Bala, about 1980, the extent of the burden carried by Elwyn in his work. He told me, with tears in his eyes, 'You now are going back to work in Bangor, but I must carry the burden and responsibility of the Movement's work every day on my own.' I saw something of the loneliness and tension and, at times, disappointment that he experienced in the work, and how it weighed very heavily upon him.

For all this, Elwyn was a help to me in so many ways while I was at Bangor – in the work of planting new Welsh-speaking churches in areas like Llangefni and Waunfawr, for example, and in developing more provision in Welsh in Bangor itself. He was zealous for all the work on the Welsh-speaking side and always longed for the Movement's work to be bilingual. He was also very supportive when I sought to lead and counsel young men who felt the call to the ministry, and would always look out for gifted individuals with a sense of calling in order to help and encourage them. He was always willing to preach for us at Bangor and to spend time in prayer with me.

(c) Elwyn's wisdom, support and prayers became even more important to me once I was appointed as Senior Lecturer (1984) and then Principal (1987) of the Theological College in Bryntirion. The situation was not at all easy. The Evangelical Movement of Wales had decided to form a new and independent Theological College, but one that also incorporated the Bible College that had been at Barry up until 1985.[3] In order to coordinate the Movement's work and to support me in my new role as the leader of the College, Elwyn was appointed as its President. This was no mere sinecure for Elwyn, even less an opportunity for him to rule the College and tell me what to do. Indeed not! Elwyn's presence was as a supporter, a close brother and a wise counsellor, who was always available for me. I spent much time in his company, in discussion but especially in prayer together. In the early years he was also available for the students and staff members. Who will forget his ministry as he preached to staff and students every September, or his important contributions in staff or Council discussions or in opening the Word at Council meetings?

I remember one occasion very clearly. The Council had before them a very important decision to make relating to the expansion of the work. On 5 December 1990, the Chairman asked Elwyn to begin the meeting. Elwyn read 1 Kings 3:1-15, James 1:5-8 and 3:13-18. He then commented on James 1:5 emphasising the promise contained in the verse and the way in which God gives wisdom to those who ask him. But he drew our attention also to verses 13-18 of the third chapter in order to describe the nature of God's wisdom and to explain how it differs from worldly wisdom. The message was immensely relevant and timely, and during the time of prayer that followed many asked for God's wisdom to be bestowed in the important discussion ahead. God answered our prayers and a clear guidance was given to the College.

I have another point to note about Elwyn. He possessed an excellent mind and considerable lecturing skills. I remember, for example, a paper he gave at a study conference of the British Evangelical Council (now Affinity) at Northampton in 1978. His subject was 'Charismatic Gifts — Today?' This theme, together with other related controversial issues, was being discussed by ministers and evangelical teachers from all parts of Britain. In particular, the question arose as to whether or not miraculous gifts and revelatory gifts could be expected today. Elwyn delivered an excellent paper of the highest standard on 1 Corinthians 13:9-12 making good use of Greek and of scholarly commentaries and showing that these verses refer, not to the period at the end of the first century when the Canon of Scripture was completed, but to heaven and glory. Here was an example of thorough, detailed and relevant study that deserves to be re-published. I refer to this occasion in order to demonstrate how much at home Elwyn was when digging deeply into the Word, discussing crucial theological subjects or the work of training ministers.

Introduction

I have by now, perhaps, commented sufficiently on Elwyn as a person, but I give thanks to God for him and for his key contribution to the Lord's work in Wales and beyond. I believe that the best way for me to express my indebtedness to him is to continue to honour the same Scriptural principles that were so important to him, and to endeavour to know God better and to experience the reviving power of his Holy Spirit in our day.

Principles
I now turn to consider four principles or doctrines that were fundamental to Elwyn in his life and work. These must of necessity be treated here very briefly, but with the purpose of re-presenting and applying them to our contemporary situation in Wales.

Are there reasons for doing this? Yes, certainly. Firstly, I have no wish to live in the past nor to labour for any cause that is past its prime! Secondly, Elwyn himself would not wish me to draw attention to himself but rather to the Scriptures, so that the Lord might receive all the attention and praise. There is no better way of doing this than to return to those Scriptural truths that were so precious to him. Thirdly, Mair Davies, his wife, has reminded us that Elwyn was 'always a man of one vision – strong in his principles, awake to any emphases that might harm the evangelical faith.'[4] This being so, it is only right to concentrate in this chapter on his key principles and attempt to expound them.

But there is another reason also. I am firmly convinced that the Scriptural doctrines that Elwyn so emphasised are still true and relevant today. Or let me state the point even more strongly. If we as Christians and churches in Wales do not take these doctrines seriously we have no right to be optimistic about the future of the church in our land.

1. The Gospel
The beginnings were fairly simple, but unexpected and critical. After being at Pen-y-groes, Caernarfonshire, collecting clothes from door to door in order to send them to Germany, Elwyn was cycling back to Caernarfon. Before reaching the town he heard an unknown voice asking him, 'Why are you doing this work?'[5] There was no other human person anywhere near him but he had no need for further explanation. He knew immediately that the Lord was speaking to him and he understood the significance of the question. At the same time, he felt a deep conviction of sin and of his own pride. 'I saw,' he said, 'the pollution of my heart

as I had never seen it before.' He was a young, religious student at the time, and in the middle of his training at Bangor for the Christian ministry and preaching regularly every Sunday.

'But the truth was,' said Elwyn, 'that I was not a Christian, and nor would I have become a Christian had I not been compelled to face up to the state of my heart, and that in the light, not of society's standards, nor of the demands of the deteriorating religion of our day, but of God's demands.'[6]

The fear of God had come upon him very suddenly and had revealed to him the emptiness of his religion and his sinfulness before the majesty of God. He felt himself a 'prisoner'[7] of sin and without hope, but also, paradoxically, he began to see the light of the gospel and 'how great was my need for that salvation which God had prepared in Jesus Christ for those like me.'[8]

God dealt with him through the following months and the crisis came at Easter 1947 at Plas-y-nant, Betws Garmon, near Caernarfon. There, at a retreat for students, he experienced at last the blessing of the grace of the gospel. By now he was, in his own words, 'more than ready to yield my life to God (for the first time, be it noted) and experience the joy of knowing not only that he had received me but that he had also forgiven all my sins.'[9]

He was now full of rejoicing, and told the lady of the house, 'God has forgiven my sins.' She did not understand what he was saying, but Elwyn never lost that assurance throughout his life.

I draw your attention to Elwyn's testimony for three reasons. In the first place, to Elwyn the gospel was unique; it was from heaven, and Scriptural. It was foundational to Christianity and therefore all-important. No compromise was possible as to the nature, the sufficiency and the message of the gospel. At the centre of the gospel was God – the Father, the Son and the Holy Spirit – who together planned and effected the salvation of sinners. To Elwyn therefore, the work of the Redeemer, as God-Man, fulfilling the law of God on our behalf and receiving our punishment upon the Cross, so purchasing our salvation, was amazing and glorious. And this is what he realized and experienced at Plas-y-nant in 1947.

Introduction

About fifty years later Elwyn wrote about the necessity for an atonement when referring to John 12:24-25,

'He [Jesus Christ] is speaking about his own death and of the fruit that shall certainly result... And that as a consequence of the grain of wheat – namely himself – falling to the ground and dying... There would be no hope for these to have life... were it not that One had died in their place, so that the penalty which they deserved for living so long for themselves, and for all their sins, was fully appropriated to, and suffered by that One instead of them.'[10] This gospel never changes!

Secondly, God not only planned and accomplished our salvation once and for ever on the Cross but he also applies it powerfully to our lives. Elwyn expressed this truth very clearly in his book *O! Ryfedd Ras [O! Wondrous Grace]*, and his words are worth quoting:

'... the Almighty God ensures that the rebellious self dies and a brand-new man, who desires from the heart to serve Jesus Christ, takes his place; the self-centred 'old man' is crucified and is resurrected a new man, eager to serve Jesus Christ. Then, to crown it all, he is 'given' to Jesus Christ to receive forgiveness of sin and to begin the most glorious knowledge and relationship that anyone can experience. This is exactly what happens when a man is born again.'[11]

Elwyn's emphasis here is the emphasis of the New Testament in its discussion of the new birth, the knowledge of God, personal and spiritual union with Christ, and the internal work of the Holy Spirit. Interestingly, when Elwyn writes of the privileges of every Christian, he refers firstly to the words of the Lord Jesus in John 17:3, emphasising that,

'Jesus Christ grants men the privilege of knowing him and, through knowing him, of knowing the Father. And this knowledge – though so amazing – proves to be as valid, living, personal and real as our knowledge of our closest friends.'[12]

But also, crowning all, 'this personal knowledge, of such extraordinary privilege, and all that it entails, will continue to all eternity!'[13]

With these words Elwyn expressed something of the depths, the excitement and the joy that he and his brothers and sisters in Christ experienced in the 1940s and 50s. Perhaps the word 'reality' describes their experience better than any other word. They were now not merely chapel-goers but the people of the Lord. Their love for him was strong and they longed to see and hear their Saviour in the Bible and to know him more. Religion alone was not now sufficient to satisfy them in that they had emerged from shadows and darkness into the glorious light of the gospel. Reality! And they were not a hard, 'separatist', 'strongly judgemental'[14] people but sheep, looking for pastors to feed and guide them. There existed some Biblical ministries in a few chapels and churches, but these were the minority.

I draw attention to Elwyn's testimony for a third reason, one that I have already referred to, namely the state of the chapels and churches of Wales at the time. Elwyn's experience, and that of many others, explains this point.

Elwyn began his spiritual pilgrimage at Pendref Congregational Chapel in Caernarfon. Though he was always glad of having been raised a chapel-goer, he confessed honestly and with sadness, 'I cannot say that I gained much from the chapel and the life of the chapel.'[15] Even when being received as a member, only matters of Congregational principles were discussed; the gospel and spiritual matters were not considered.

Elwyn's reminiscences provide a picture of the spiritual state of the churches at that time. One of his chapel's deacons, for example, very openly denied orthodox beliefs such as the resurrection of the Lord Jesus and his miracles. Good Friday would be a day for holding an *eisteddfod* (cultural festival) without any thought of meeting for a communion service or to remember the Cross! But one member, Mair Jones, stood out because of her personal faith in Christ, her kindness, and her experience of the Holy Spirit. When she took part in the weekly prayer meeting 'her face shone. You felt that she was speaking with someone she loved – to take part in the meeting had no sense of formality for her.' Though she was so godly, said Elwyn, 'I'm sure she was quite lonely from a spiritual point of view.' And this was the experience of many Christians in Wales.

But what had happened to the chapels? Without the members fully realising it, 'liberal theology', according to Emyr Roberts, had, at the beginning of the twentieth century, 'come in as a strong flood and had in time possessed the land.'[16] The result? By the 1930s, he continued,

Introduction

'the Protestant, evangelical doctrine that had been such a power in our land for nearly two centuries had been laid aside almost completely.'[17] This is not merely the personal opinion of Emyr Roberts; the truth stated is acknowledged by many scholars including R. Tudur Jones, D. Densil Morgan and Robert Pope. For example, in his chapter on 'Helynt Tom Nefyn yn y Tymbl [Tom Nefyn's Troubles in Tumble]' from 1925 onwards, Pope emphasises that, 'Theological Modernism, with its emphasis on the application of the moral principles of the gospel, was common enough by that time.'[18] In another chapter he refers to one aspect of the effect of the theological liberalism on the doctrines of the denominations:

'... by 1904, it is clear that the traditional understandings of the Atonement and the substitutionary death of Jesus, and the teaching that his sacrifice was valid in that he was "true God and true man", were moving towards a Christian understanding that considered Jesus in terms of the perfect humanity expressed by his complete obedience to the will of God and his filial awareness of his heavenly Father... his death was to be understood as a moral self-sacrifice.'[19]

These unscriptural doctrines had enormous and tragic effect upon the life, membership and work of the chapels in Wales. It is in this context that I refer to the way in which Elwyn understood the theological liberalism of his youth.

For example, his grandfather owned Matthew Henry's Bible Commentary as well as Thomas Scott's valuable five-volumed commentary on the Bible. But Elwyn 'felt nervous' of reading these books because the comments that he had heard with respect to the orthodox faith were 'so sweeping, so disparaging...'[20] As a student preparing for the ministry he realised that it was taken for granted that no-one could now believe these orthodox truths and that 'everything was presented in terms of scholarship.'[21] The tendency of many of the chapel leaders and College lecturers was towards an intolerant harshness as they defended and presented their theological liberalism.

It was sad to read Elwyn's account of his meeting with the Rev. George M. Ll. Davies, a minister with the Presbyterians and a famous Welsh pacifist, but a man who had turned away from the orthodox Faith (see *Cyrraedd Trwy'r Glustog*, 50-54). They met on the train, near Llandudno, and Elwyn explained that he and his friend had been taking part in an evangelistic campaign at Llanfairfechan. When the old minister heard of their work in the campaign, he responded very humbly:

'Well done, boys,' he said. 'At the end of my journey I have had to come back to something that was said to me when I was very young.' He referred to someone who had explained to him 'the ABC of Christianity': 'All have sinned; Behold the Lamb of God; Come unto Me'. Elwyn added his own comment, '... he was explaining to us that he had left the ABC but at the end of his life was having to admit his mistake and to return to this point.'[22]

Whatever might be said for theological liberalism in its various branches and developments, one thing is certain: ultimately, it undermines and conceals the historic, orthodox Faith; indeed, it denies it. Early in the 1970s, Professor Bobi Jones, Aberystwyth, stated: 'Heresy was the normal state of affairs... Those who uphold the Unfeigned Faith in Wales today are very few.' The point is also underlined by another Aberystwyth-based professor, R. Geraint Gruffydd: 'In my experience, at least, very little of this [proclaiming the Gospel] is heard from the pulpits and ecclesiastical courts of the Church in Wales, the Methodists, the Congregationalists, and so on...'[23] I emphasise this because it is not fair to describe Elwyn and the supporters of the Movement as hard and 'separatist'. The main reason for their separation was this: for them, the gospel meant everything. If the denominations had kept faithfully to the gospel and the orthodox Faith, they would not have felt any need to leave their chapels and establish evangelical churches. In the end it was a matter of necessity and of urgency, in order that the gospel might be consistently proclaimed, congregations taught and that believers might know unity and fellowship. Some evangelicals were perhaps unwise and lacking in patience at times in their response to denominations or local churches, especially so in the seventies, and I acknowledge the fact. But the mistakes at the time do not change the main reason for their secession, namely, teachings that fudged and denied the eternal gospel. Certainly Lloyd-Jones supported them in many ways, but in particular he underlined for them the answers to two basic and foundational questions with respect to the nature of the church and the definition of a Christian. But above everything else, it was the unspiritual state of the chapels that drove them out to form evangelical churches.

Before leaving this principle, it is appropriate for me to refer to the addresses Elwyn delivered at a Ministers' Conference in Bala in 1972.

Introduction

His topic was 'The Biblical Doctrine of Error.'[24] Without doubt this was a masterly, scholarly and very relevant contribution.

He distinguished between four groups of people who, according to the Scriptures, may be in error: those who do not understand God's Word and ways correctly; those who err in spirit and at heart; those guilty of false witness; and, fourthly, those who live in a state of error (2 Peter 3:17-18; 1 John 4:6). I draw attention to this last group, in particular, in order to explain, to some extent, the response of some evangelicals who separated from their churches in the 1960s and 1970s.

By quoting and expounding relevant texts from Scripture (Rom. 16:17; 1 Tim. 6:3-5; 2 Tim. 3:5; Tit. 3:10) Elwyn proceeded to show why the false teachers of the Early Church were so dangerous, and why it was necessary to deal firmly with them. He gave five reasons from Scripture.

Firstly, they were following their own ideas and philosophies and not God's Word (Col. 2:8, 20-22; Tit. 1:14). Secondly, they were denying the Faith – not denying one part of the truth only but departing from the doctrines of the Word comprehensively (2 Cor. 10:11-13; Gal. 1:7; 1 Tim. 6:3; 2 Tim. 3:8; Tit. 1:13). Thirdly, their false teaching leads to ungodliness (Phil. 3:18-19; 1 Tim. 6:5; 2 Tim. 2:16, 3:5; 2 Peter 2; Jude), and fourthly, they are ultimately Satan's servants (Rom. 16:17-20; 2 Cor. 10:12). Lastly, they are dangerous because they are not always easy to recognise (Matt. 7:15; Acts 20:29-30; 1 John 2:19). For these reasons, therefore, the Church must bear its responsibility for warning and disciplining them.

As a consequence, and unlike the majority of church and chapel members at the time, evangelicals acknowledged the Scriptures as their main authority in all matters of faith and conduct. And, by God's grace, they discovered in the Scriptures the glorious and heavenly gospel. This principle is all-important, not only for understanding the work of Elwyn Davies, but for understanding the new movement that brought many Christians out of their chapels into new evangelical churches. The gospel was their predominant concern. Interestingly, when Lloyd-Jones died in 1981, Elwyn acknowledged his appreciation of his contribution during the first years of the Movement:

'Had Dr Lloyd-Jones not been with us at that time, there is little doubt that the work of the gospel in Wales would have taken a very different form.'[25]

23

2. *Spirituality*

The word 'spirituality' has a contemporary ring to it and it has gathered a wide range of meanings expressing every kind of secular and religious idea from many countries. But when considering Christian spirituality we are rightly reminded by Alister E. McGrath of the necessary connection between orthodox doctrines and practice ('*praxis'*).[26] Spirituality focuses on that which an individual does with his faith in his life and community. How may we understand Elwyn's spirituality? It belongs to the reformed tradition in Wales with its Biblical roots in the Nonconformity of the eighteenth and nineteenth centuries. This is the period in Wales when denominations such as the Calvinistic Methodists, the Congregationalists and the Baptists were faithful to the doctrines of the Word but emphasised at the same time the necessity of knowing God, of experiencing the power of the Holy Spirit personally and within their churches, and of endeavouring to live holy and Christ-centred lives. We can be more specific in describing this spirituality. The following elements, for example, were basic and all-important: the authority of the Bible as the infallible Word of God; preaching, reading and understanding the Word; the re-birth, conversion, spiritual union with Christ, prayer and fellowship with other Christians at the local church level – and all in the context of a loving and close relationship with the Lord and a commitment to him. This was exactly the spirituality that was Elwyn's.

For him, God's Word was a priceless treasure; it was food and medicine to the soul, a loving letter from his Beloved. It was also a living book, authoritative, exciting and dynamic, in which the Lord would speak to him and meet with him. He found great pleasure and satisfaction in his continual reading and meditating in the Word. This is confirmed by Professor R. Geraint Gruffydd, a close friend of Elwyn's for many years:

'Elwyn's greatest delight always was meditating upon the message of the Bible — particularly that of his favourite Gospel of John — and then sharing the fruit of his meditations to as many people as wished to hear him.'[27]

Elwyn himself underlines for us the importance of the Bible, meditation and the means of grace if we wish for a better understanding and knowledge of God. By meditation, we 'use our minds to the utmost of our ability, and give ourselves to meditate on the great truths of which we already possess some measure of understanding.'[28] But in addition, he emphasised that we should 'make use of the means which the Holy

24

Introduction

Spirit has provided for a wider grasp of the truth. The Bible – reading it often; listening to sermons; expecting to receive a better understanding of truth whoever it is who is preaching; the experiences of the saints; reading of that which was revealed to them from the Word; singing the great hymns – hymns of great doctrinal content; praying together, at which times God usually reveals great things of himself to those who seek him.'

Elwyn also realised the absolute necessity of the work of the Holy Spirit in re-creating sinners in Christ. In his lecture, 'Epistemeg Gristnogol [Christian Epistemology]', given in 1979, he emphasised from Scripture that every person, because of sin, is naturally an enemy of God, blind to the things of the spirit, captive to sin and spiritually dead. This is the effect of the Fall upon us all. But there is a remedy to be found at the Cross, and he wrote: 'The Almighty God is able to re-create men from within, as it were, changing them completely spiritually, removing the poison of their hatred of God from their veins, planting a new spirit within them – regenerating them.'[29] To become a Christian is not something emotional, or human, or easy. It is a miracle; it is the supernatural work of the Holy Spirit changing individuals from the inside. This became a fact and a reality in Elwyn's life when he was a student at Bangor. And his great desire from then on, in order to please his Saviour, was to live obediently to the Word. His integrity, in all areas of life, was of the highest. This is why Idris Charles has recently written of him:

'I can say that to this day I have never experienced such spiritual company than that of Mr Davies. For me, all that I knew of Jesus Christ radiated through him. His love for me and influence upon me was very great.'[30]

And there are very many people of all ages and over a long period of time who would have similar testimonies of him.

Prayer was at the heart of Elwyn's life; he was essentially a praying man, and this was the secret of his consistently close walk with God.

Mair has reminded us of some of the things he said about prayer. For example, the Lord Jesus spent hours in prayer to his heavenly Father, even in the midst of the busyness of his ministry, and to Elwyn the Lord's pattern required that all Christians should also give time to prayer and to the expression of dependence upon God and appreciation of his fellowship. Prayer also is the means of asking – as Elwyn so often did – for the knowledge of God's will in a particular situation. 'He admired the WEC [Worldwide Evangelisation Crusade]'[31] wrote Mair, 'because they set aside a day of prayer before holding a meeting.'[32]

In this context, he laid great stress on 'praying in His name'. This was not a formal action but a matter of seeking God himself and finding liberty to plead and to receive an assurance that what was being sought had been obtained. Elwyn gave a definition of 'praying in His name' in his book *O! Ryfedd Ras*, namely, 'praying in accordance with his will, his commandments and words.'[33]

One example of this made a great impression on Elwyn, and he often spoke to me of the occasion. Let me give the background. I received an invitation to lead the new College at Bryntirion in October 1984. I asked if I might take some weeks to think and pray before responding because there was one matter that was causing me considerable concern. At the next Council it was clear that I could not respond positively, and I said as much. The Council members were disappointed and so, on their behalf, Elwyn asked me to reconsider, and to meet with him and another individual the next morning. I agreed at last, but the situation the next day had not changed in any way, and for about two hours the discussion was honest but unpleasant. Suddenly, about half past eleven, the other person's attitude changed completely and wonderfully. It seemed like a miracle.

I returned to Bangor, and late that night the Rev. Arthur Neil, a Baptist pastor in England, phoned me. He knew nothing of my situation or need, but his first question was: 'What was happening to you this morning?' Before I had time to reply he said, 'I was preparing a sermon this morning, and suddenly I was burdened to pray for you. I continued for half an hour in earnest prayer but at about half past eleven I was assured that the Lord had heard my prayer for you and that you were free to do that which you are meant to do, whatever it is.' When I shared this with Elwyn later, he rejoiced and marvelled. Many times afterwards he mentioned the occasion to me. 'That was a prayer in the name of the Lord Jesus,' he said, 'and we must pray more in His name, just like Arthur Neil.' To pray in this way was a thrilling and powerful experience for Elwyn, and he himself often experienced similar answers.

Introduction

At the Ministers' Conference at Bala in June 1982, Elwyn had the privilege and responsibility of delivering the closing address before everyone returned to their homes and churches. He chose Luke 11:1-13 as his text, and asked the key questions, 'How may we become men who are diligent in prayer?' and 'How may we become persevering and fervent in our prayers?' For an answer, he gave four comments on the text.[34]

He firstly emphasised the fact that prayer means so much more than merely asking God for things. He referred to the first and second verses of Luke 11 to underline the nature of the things for which the Lord tells us to pray. But, said Elwyn, the Lord does not promise that merely to ask will obtain answers; there is also a responsibility laid upon us to seek and to knock on heaven's door for these things.

Secondly, there is no true fervency in prayer unless we truly long for the Lord's name to be exalted and for his kingdom to come in power.

Thirdly, we must remind ourselves that God is very willing that we should experience great things in prayer. He quoted verses 9 and 10 to prove the point. The promise is given to every Christian, and God will not mock them. We should therefore recognise his willingness to give us good things, but realise also that there is a need for us to seek them earnestly. This is our duty and our privilege, but, unfortunately, this is where we tend to give up without having sought diligently.

Fourthly, it is not possible to persevere in prayer if we do not believe that the Lord is with us to help us. The Holy Spirit will lead us and enable us to pray. We must persevere! Elwyn's message was very challenging but it revealed also the vital importance which prayer held for him, and his burden for seeing ministers praying effectively.

Another characteristic of Elwyn's spirituality that deserves to be noted here was his commitment to the Redeemer. He gave himself to Him fully and completely. Let me give just the one example – one that formed a considerable challenge to the readers of Y Cylchgrawn Efengylaidd.[35] Elwyn wrote an article for that periodical in 1956 on a basic and practical theme, namely, 'Gwrthgilwyr Diarwybod' ['Unwitting Backsliders']. He took for granted the Scriptural truth that Christians love God but, very soon in the article, he proceeded to ask two questions to prove the reality and strength of their love for God. The first was: 'Do you love God

with all your heart, and with all your soul, and with all your strength.'[36]
He further asks, 'Do you or I know something of *this* love towards God in
these days? ... Is it something occasional, weak and of feeble influence?'
He suggests that we as Christians have lost the thrill and reality of our
love to our Lord. The article then proceeds to describe three types of
Christian today.[37] 'Firstly, it must be acknowledged that a large class of
believers... have to all intents and purposes denied their profession and
returned to the world.' A further class is that of 'unwitting backsliders':
externally the members of this class read their Bibles, 'pray, witness,
tithe, attend services regularly... they are children of God, *but have
backslidden from him.*'

But how did that happen? His answer is that we are guilty of being
careless of our fellowship with God and with his Son Jesus Christ. Our
greatest sin therefore is of neglecting God himself, and we have a
responsibility of returning to him in repentance, and of giving the first
place in our hearts to him. The members of the third class always put
God first. Nothing can persuade these to 'neglect the hour of prayer' nor
their fellowship with him.

Elwyn appealed before concluding for us to return to God: 'to give
ourselves fully to him, not, in the first place, to serve him, but to him,
to his fellowship... We must insist on giving priority, before all other
things, to God, and we will find that our spiritual lives will be renewed
thoroughly. Our *love* for him will return; our love for men and women
will also return.'

We see here that Elwyn's spirituality was Biblical, prayerful, moral and
practical, but also dynamic and experimental, flowing from a close
relationship with Christ and the Holy Spirit. He has much to teach us
and to challenge us regarding Christian spirituality.

3. Christian and church unity
It might be possible superficially to interpret Elwyn's attitude to Christian
and church unity purely in terms of the influence of Dr Martyn Lloyd-
Jones. Elwyn was, indeed, a close friend of 'the Doctor' for many years,
and faithful to him to the end. He admired him as a preacher, pastor,
theologian, counsellor and Welsh-speaking Welshman. It is true also that
Martyn Lloyd-Jones had introduced very many young ministers in Wales
to reformed theology, especially in the 1950s and 1960s. This occurred

Introduction

very clearly in the Welsh IVF Conferences at Borth near Aberystwyth in the early fifties, where Elwyn himself received much blessing and was convicted that these doctrines were Scriptural and also part of our tradition in Wales. Martyn Lloyd-Jones contributed substantially again in the sixties by explaining the nature and unity of the Church and the significance of schism. His London address on this theme in 1966 was at the invitation of the National Assembly of Evangelicals. He was asked by the Assembly's committee to repeat the address he had given to them.

This 1966 Assembly address will always be remembered. His contribution was historical, challenging and controversial and proved a turning point in the history of evangelicals in England and Wales. Elwyn and other people in Wales agreed with Lloyd-Jones, and he was only expressing thoughts that Elwyn had himself wrestled with and had argued for. Undoubtedly, Elwyn was greatly stimulated and challenged by considering 'the Doctor's' message on the nature and unity of the Church.

However, while this is true, I disagree with the criticism sometimes heard that Elwyn and other evangelicals in Wales followed Lloyd-Jones like sheep, without thinking for themselves. That was not true at all. What was true was that both Elwyn and Lloyd-Jones had reached a similar understanding as to the nature of the Church but by different paths. I will argue this point in more detail elsewhere,[38] but would like to present and apply here that which Elwyn taught about unity on four levels, so that there might be no danger of misunderstanding or of hiding behind ambiguous words.

(a) The first level of Christian unity is, of course, love between Christians, and between Christians of different denominations, countries and backgrounds.

After his conversion in 1947, Elwyn realised increasingly that he had brothers and sisters in Christ. It is no wonder that Noel Gibbard could state: 'Back in Bangor Elwyn Davies and others felt an ever-deepening desire for more fellowship with those of like belief and experience.'[39] This was no narrow desire to form a clique nor part of a campaign to shut other people out, but a radical response resulting from the supernatural work of the Holy Spirit (Galatians 5:22-23) in his life. By quoting John 13:34-35, Elwyn emphasised that Christians, at all times and in all places, had the responsibility of loving one another.[40] He himself was a striking example of this in many ways.

(b) The second level of Christian unity is the fact that every Christian is a member of the Church.

This is an evident and Scriptural truth but Elwyn issued the strong warning, 'We make this our starting point. To belong to the body of Christ, one has first to belong to Christ. It is such people, and only such, who constitute the body of Christ.'[41] Some of our denominations in Wales stood for this truth in the past, but do not do so to the same extent today. Elwyn himself, for example, was fourteen years of age when he became a member of Pendref Chapel, Caernarfon. His comment on that event was: 'There was no examining of one's experience as to whether we believed or not, and as to how we might know.'[42] He was 'taking the steps' of being accepted but, he said, 'the gospel itself was far from being involved.' And this also was my experience in a different denomination. But the true church, according to the New Testament, is composed only of believers, that is, of those who have been regenerated and who know the Saviour. They alone make up the body of Christ (1 Cor. 12:27; 1:2).[43]

(c) The next level of the doctrine to which Elwyn held follows from those discussed above, namely that true Christian unity is not between denominations but across denominations.

This was his experience as a student and for many years in the ministry. One of the reasons why the Evangelical Movement of Wales arranged many *seiat* meetings[44] throughout Wales in the 1950s and 1960s was his concern for providing Biblical teaching and fellowship for Christians from various denominations within their own localities, when no consistent Biblical ministry or opportunity to fellowship with other Christians was available for them in their own churches. For the same reason the Movement, in 1967, also arranged fraternal societies for evangelical ministers from different denominations. They experienced a deep unity together, but it was an unity across denominations and in the gospel and its truths.

(d) In order to explain this point further, let me emphasise a further level in Elwyn's teaching, namely his unhappiness, with good reason, with plans to unite some denominations in Wales.

Many events that occurred in 1962-63 resulted in it being a key period with respect to ecumenism. Sir David James offered a generous monetary gift on condition that the Welsh Nonconformist denominations united within a short period of time. The offer was unexpected and challenging, but on the whole the churches responded positively. There was also a sense of excitement and expectation amongst church leaders and members. The four denominations published a plan in 1963, *Towards Unity*, and a more ambitious and detailed one in 1965, *Plan of Union: the United Church of Wales*. Not everyone was happy with these developments, the evangelicals in particular. But Dr Martyn Lloyd-Jones wished for the churches to unite! A surprising response? Let 'the Doctor' explain:

'... my belief is that all the denominations (including the episcopal Church) should unite at once, as there is nothing of importance separating them in teaching or doctrine! But, on exactly the same basis, you cannot expect those who disagree with them on essential and basic questions be a part of that united church.'[45]

He continued by discussing important issues involved in the concept of the united church being considered, matters such as authority, tradition and belief.

Elwyn responded to the plan, *Towards Unity*, on behalf of the Movement in a pamphlet, *The United Church of Wales*.[46] His response was detailed, sensitive and theological, and he foresaw danger in the forming of a new church. Why? The first reason he gave is unexpected: the plan had not considered what it was that the denominations should yield in order to unite. But a second, more important reason for him, was the failure to express and justify the plan in the light of the Bible as the main authority in matters of faith and practice. At the end of the pamphlet, Elwyn suggested 'the only answer' to the church situation, namely for the denominations to return to the New Testament and to reform themselves, in thought and in behaviour.

According to Professor Densil Morgan, the attitudes of Lloyd-Jones and the Movement towards ecumenism had hardened considerably by 1962.[47] Later he emphasises this point even more strongly. By the middle of the sixties, he states, the expression of evangelicalism from the Movement's point of view was tending towards Calvinism and 'separatist and... strongly judgemental of other forms of Christian faith.'[48] Was this true? Certainly Professor Morgan refers here to a perception held by many but his interpretation of the Movement's response between 1962 and 1965 is questionable. In order to understand 1962 correctly it is essential that we remind ourselves of the background, which was vital to the question. No-one will be able to understand the attitude of the Welsh evangelicals towards church unity without appreciating the background and events that led up to 1962. In this context I want to consider four points.

Firstly, it is important to provide some historical background in order to understand the situation that faced the evangelicals in the 50s and 60s. The World Council of Churches had been established in 1948 in Amsterdam, and then the Welsh Council of Churches in 1956.[49] The four denominations, namely the Church in Wales, the Methodist Church of Great Britain, the Presbyterian Church of Wales, the United Reformed Church of England and Wales – together with some local Baptist churches – agreed to covenant towards the forming of a new mutual relationship, with the ultimate purpose of forming a united Church. There was pressure therefore on churches and on evangelicals also to be part of this ecumenical movement.

Noel Davies emphasises the fact that local co-operation had prepared the way for the formation of the Welsh Council of Churches[50] and, by 1969, sixty local Councils had become members. In some areas the local Council of Churches worked very effectively and in many different ways. In the Llynfi Valley in the sixties, for example, where I ministered, the Council of Churches arranged a number of events. In one part of the Valley (Caerau) nearly all the churches agreed to celebrate Whit Sunday with a procession through the streets of the village followed by an open-air meeting. However, not only the chapels and the Church in Wales took part but also a group of Spiritists! One thing is certain: there was considerable pressure on churches and evangelicals to be part of the ecumenical movement at the local, national and international levels. This, therefore, was an important factor in forcing evangelicals to reconsider the Scriptural doctrines on the nature of the church and its relation to the denominations.

Secondly, there was another movement, a spiritual and exciting movement, active in Wales and in Britain during the forties, fifties and sixties. The following are some of the words we might use to describe accurately the unexpected but powerful events that occurred at that time in Wales amongst Christians of different denominations – life; blessing; persevering prayer; power; zeal; never-to-be-forgotten meetings; expectation; and disappointment also.

Life? Yes, certainly. It is impossible to sum up all the people both in the Colleges and outside who were saved between 1947 and 1962. There was a tremendous blessing on the Word in the Colleges, in preaching services, in fruitful campaigns in towns like Bala and Llanelli, in children's and young people's camps from 1954 onwards, and also in the Magazine, Movement and IVF Conferences. Blessing is the only appropriate word for describing the first years of the Movement. Power accompanied some of the preachers at this time. This was Calvinism on fire! But what of the disappointment? The answer to that question is considered in the next section.

Thirdly, the rise of the Ecumenical Movement, particularly at local and national levels, drove the leaders of the Evangelical Movement and the Welsh ministers in their fraternals to consider, as a matter of urgency, the nature of the church. The Movement published many pamphlets before presenting *The Christian Church* in 1966.[51] This was a booklet describing the authority and nature of the church according to the New Testament. It emphasised the authority and sufficiency of the Scriptures and the fact that members of the churches should be those who are born again. No-one in the Evangelical Movement would have claimed that it was infallible, as Noel Gibbard underlines when quoting from it:

'If in any way at all we have strayed from the teaching of the Bible, then we invite our readers to inform us – and we trust we shall have the grace to be corrected. It is the desire to honour God by obeying Him that moves us.'[52]

But the preparing of that booklet had involved prayerful, detailed, hard work by many over a long period. These included many ministers in their fraternals and at ministers' conferences at Bala. I emphasise this point in order to demonstrate that the Movement had studied doctrines such as the nature of the church for nearly three years before October 1966, when Lloyd-Jones gave his historical address in London. The Welsh did not depend on 'the Doctor'. Nor did Welsh evangelicals react immediately or hastily without careful consideration.

Fourthly, although some evangelicals had separated from their denominations, others had remained, but continued as supporters of the Evangelical Movement. At times there were tensions, with some individuals reacting ungraciously and unwisely towards brethren. There is no excuse for this at all, and I do not condone such behaviour. On the other hand, there were very many men both within and without the denominations who maintained a close and sincere fellowship. Many who had left encouraged their brethren in practical ways by preaching in their denominational churches and supporting them. This is something that Elwyn continued to do over the years, and the Evangelical Movement was committed strongly to such unity in the gospel.

(e) The last point that I wish to stress is the fact that evangelical unity was all-important to Elwyn and to the Movement.

Mair, Elwyn's wife, said of him: 'He worked selflessly for this aim. There should be no separation, he would say, over secondary issues. He always dealt very fairly with brethren in the denominational churches. He wished all to be in agreement.'

The book that Elwyn wrote on unity, *Striving Together*, deserves to be much better known by Christians although parts of it are dated. It is a small book of 56 pages that amply repays any time and study given to it.

Firstly, in my opinion, this is one of the most important books that Elwyn wrote, and perhaps the most important book published by the Movement, certainly the most important in the 1980s. The book's significance is to be seen in the way it summarises the history of the Movement within the context of the churches in Wales. It then proceeds to highlight some Biblical principles in order to apply them to the complex religious situation and to give clear guidance to evangelicals.

It is an important book for another reason also. Though the contemporary scene has changed since the eighties, its argument still remains very relevant and challenging with respect to Christian and church unity. Not so much now in terms of evangelicals separating from denominations but of evangelicals separating from one another, because of secondary issues or even because of personal matters. This is where Elwyn's book challenges us all to think and act on the basis of Scripture and not on secondary matters.

To help us to do this, Elwyn concentrates on the basic Biblical principles relating to the church and to unity. For example, after explaining what the church, or the Body of Christ, is, he emphasises that we are all one in the Lord, having a responsibility to demonstrate our unity to the world

(John 17:17, 21, 23). Too often we show the world our divisions rather than our unity.[53] But what of our disagreements? Elwyn was again a realist in his approach to the problem. Instead of breaking fellowship with other evangelical churches, he emphasised the need to respect one another and to remember that we all belong to the same family, God's family. Part of our responsibility also is to do all within our powers, in love and respect, to help one another as churches to understand and obey the Word further.[54] In addition, Elwyn accepted Lloyd-Jones' interpretation of the word 'schism' in 1 Corinthians 12: 25. It is only Christians that can be guilty of this sin, not through leaving denominational churches but through separating from their brothers and sisters in Christ.[55]

It is an important book, therefore, and deserves to be edited, and read again by a new generation of Christians. What the book does, of course, is to express the burden that Elwyn felt for unity between Christians and evangelical churches. He often gave his time and energies to ponder these things, and he prayed consistently for true unity and love to be maintained.

In 1967, the Evangelical Movement became a member of the British Evangelical Council (BEC),[56] and between 1969 and 1972 Elwyn served as its President. This position involved him in considerably more work and much travelling also, but he carried it out willingly 'because evangelical unity had such a place in his heart at all times,' said Mair. 'One question that he often asked was, "Why should brethren separate?" '

Why did the Movement join the BEC? There were many reasons, but two are relevant here. One reason was the opportunity that doing so gave of consulting and co-operating with other church leaders and evangelical denominations in Britain, so that the churches might learn from one another.[57] The second reason is more basic, namely that it provided the opportunity to demonstrate as wide a unity as possible, but on the basis of the Scriptures being their supreme authority in all matters of faith and practice. Elwyn was held in the highest regard by leaders and churches within the BEC for his vision and concern, as well as for his wisdom and ability to think clearly and theologically from the Word.

We have much to learn today within our churches and across churches of true unity. There are profound challenges for us to face if we are to put into operation the principles that were so important to Elwyn.

4. Revival

Easter 1947 and January 1948 were very important dates in Elwyn's life and in the history of contemporary evangelicalism in Wales. With the help of others he had arranged a retreat in Plas-y-nant, Betws Garmon, near Caernarfon, for Bangor students. It was then that Elwyn and two others were converted. The words of the verse, 1 Corinthians 15:34 came back to him, but in this case with deep conviction. Before the end of the retreat, he had experienced complete forgiveness and great joy in the Lord. During the following weeks, many Bangor students were born again, and it was an encouraging time.

All unknown to him, there was a further period of particular blessing awaiting him. It began unexpectedly at the following retreat in January 1948. Before describing this retreat, I wish to distinguish between the ordinary work of the Holy Spirit and his extraordinary work, as this will provide the theological framework by which to understand and appreciate what happened to Elwyn, and why he had such a burden for revival.

Regeneration is part of the ordinary work of the Holy Spirit, and he subsequently lives within every Christian, strengthening and enabling him to know his Saviour better and to obey him. In prayer also, or when reading the Word, the Holy Spirit ministers to Christians. The ordinary work of the Spirit is therefore a continuing work – no-one can become a Christian, or continue a Christian, without his work and power.

Elwyn consistently emphasised this: the importance and fruit of our indwelling by the Spirit. In an address at the Ministers' Conference at Bala in 1991, for example, when discussing the subject, 'worshipping in Spirit and in Truth' he referred to the results of regeneration: '...we must insist that regeneration has continuing spiritual consequences... the spiritual life that Jesus Christ gives to men rises to the surface at all times... the fountain planted within us by the Lord Jesus Christ supplies its streams continuously. It is a fountain.' He later added, 'it is essential to realise that we are completely dependent upon the Holy Spirit.' Quoting John 7:37-39 and 14:16-18, he said, 'The Holy Spirit within us is the most important element... the Holy Spirit within us is responsible for the fact that the fountain continues to maintain its streams...' This is true for every Christian and is part of the Spirit's ordinary work.

But in addition, the Holy Spirit may work in a most powerful way. There are differences between the ordinary and the extraordinary work of the Spirit but they are differences only of degree, not of essence. And this is what occurred at that second retreat for young people at Ty'n-y-coed,[58] Dolgellau, January 1948.

The main speaker at the Conference was the Rev. T. Arthur Pritchard, and in his diary he noted the developing nature of the retreat. A great hardness prevailed with little freedom for the speaker during the first day and a half. Mr Pritchard felt driven to pray for some hours on the Saturday morning. On the Monday morning the prayer meeting was a good meeting and it was evident that prayer was a central feature of the retreat. Some were converted after being convicted of sin. Up to this point the Holy Spirit was clearly present in his ordinary work, converting some and granting freedom and help in prayer to the preacher and his friends. This is what the Spirit does continually, but there was an extra dimension also present at that retreat. One entry, for example, in Arthur Pritchard's diary reads: 'The Holy Spirit fell in a remarkable way, the atmosphere changed,' on the Saturday afternoon, and on the Sunday: 'great things happened there...'

But after finishing his Monday morning address on Romans 6, he was unable to find the words to describe the subsequent events:

'It is difficult to find the words to express what happened at the end of the service; the Holy Spirit fell in a wonderful way upon the company. A new and strange experience, a day that I shall always remember...'

This was an example of the extraordinary work of the Holy Spirit.

It was not revival, yet it was a foretaste of what the Lord does in a revival, and a deep and thrilling experience of the power and might of the Holy Spirit. In a revival, of course, Christians are quickened to an even further extent, and many more unbelievers are saved in a short time. This can happen at any time in any service; it may be limited to one chapel, village or locality, or it may spread over a whole country. The Lord in his sovereignty decides where, when and to what degree the Holy Spirit falls in power upon his people.

What is of importance and interest for us to notice is this. Although Elwyn and the brethren had not experienced revival, they had received a taste of it, that is, of the extraordinary work of the Spirit. This is a dimension that very few Christians today know of, nor indeed anticipate, sad to say. But after having experienced it, Elwyn and the others had, over the years, a desire and burden for the Lord to visit us in power again in Wales, so that the Lord Jesus might be exalted. Mair confirms this: 'He never forgot this emphasis.' And he would read extensively of the revivals of the past, particularly those in Wales.

This is why Elwyn would go to Cwm-twrch, in the Swansea valley, every Friday morning in the 1960s, to meet with Pastor George Griffiths and other ministers in order to pray for an awakening. For the same reason also he would lead days or mornings of prayer for ministers in Bryntirion for many years during the 1980s and 1990s. He longed ardently for the Lord to visit Wales once more.

There were further occasions, after the Dolgellau retreat of 1948, when Elwyn and his fellow ministers experienced that dimension of the extraordinary work of the Spirit: during some campaigns, conferences, prayer meetings, and during his own ministry. Thus, for example, after being ordained as minister of Jerusalem Congregational Chapel, Blaenau Ffestiniog, quite a large church, in September 1950, he experienced a period of blessing in 1954 and 1955 amongst the young people. Again, during the first English Conference of the Movement in 1957 in Sandfields, there was great blessing under the ministry of Lloyd-Jones. 'The Doctor' had to leave early to get back to London and Elwyn took his place for the last meeting. 'Tell them of what happened at Dolgellau,' was Lloyd-Jones' advice. Elwyn did so, with the result that, 'God's presence was as a weight upon the congregation and all were unwilling to leave at the end.'

Conclusions

Before concluding these remarks on revival, I shall make some practical comments in order to summarise the message of this introduction and also to provide a guide for forming our own response in our contemporary situation to the Word and to the example and teaching of Elwyn Davies.

(a) Firstly, there is a close and inseparable relationship between the gospel and the ordinary and extraordinary work of the Holy Spirit.

This was an important truth for Elwyn and it remains important for the Evangelical Movement and for evangelical churches today. Commenting on 1

Introduction

Peter 1:23, Elwyn wrote, 'Through the same gospel that the Lord Jesus Christ proclaimed to Nicodemus, God regenerates men: through "the foolishness of the message preached", as the Apostle Paul has it, the miracle takes place. That is how important the gospel is, and how critically important the act of proclaiming it.'[59]

We may express this principle in a negative way also. That is, the Holy Spirit never blesses heresy, or any other theology that is not Scriptural and Christ-centred. In God's order of things this is inevitable and reasonable. God's Word 'is truth' (John 17:17) that was revealed by God himself and written down infallibly by the Holy Spirit through the instrumentality of various authors over many centuries. The Bible is not merely of interest in the tradition of the church, it means so much more. It is God's Word, an infallible Word, a unique Word, which is 'living and active' (Hebrews 4: 12). This Word is, and must be, the supreme authority for the Church in all matters of faith and practice. And at the heart of the Bible, running through it as a golden thread, is the gospel. Is it not reasonable therefore that it is only that Word written by himself, and that Saviour presented in the Word, that the Holy Spirit blesses? Glorifying Christ is the work of the Holy Spirit (John 16:14) and, consequently, if we wish for blessing in our churches the necessary condition is that we believe and preach God's Word.

Lloyd-Jones confirms this point strongly and in detail: 'the great need is for forceful, convicting preaching, in the power of the Holy Spirit, proclaiming judgement, calling for repentance, offering free salvation through the blood of Christ, justification by faith alone, and the miraculous rebirth. These truths must be believed and held with assurance before we can begin to pray for that outpouring of the Holy Spirit which alone can enable us to stem the threatening floods...'[60]

Elwyn Davies would have agreed wholeheartedly.

(b) Secondly, there is a close and inseparable relationship between revival and the work of evangelism.

We see this in the history of the Evangelical Movement of Wales in the 1940s and 1950s particularly. God met with those who had gathered at Dolgellau and other places, and as a consequence they were on fire for the gospel and for reaching people with the gospel. They were not mere 'activists', but those who knew God and loved him with all their hearts and all their strength.

For example, some months after the Dolgellau retreat, a campaign was held at Bala. The week was full of prayer meetings and preaching, with some of the young Christians testifying, and singing to the harp. It was not easy to begin with; however, on the third night there was blessing, and then, 'in the fourth meeting the floodgates opened.' Noel Gibbard describes what happened:

'The Holy Spirit worked powerfully on the hearts of many. They were convicted of sin but they now needed to be directed to Christ. A further meeting was arranged for the troubled seekers...'[61]

What were the effects of that night?

'The whole area was electrified by the news.' writes Noel Gibbard, 'The mighty were brought low and the weak uplifted; prominent men of the town were not ashamed to witness for their Saviour... '

As there is such a close link between evangelising and the work of the Holy Spirit, we do not have the right to choose between them. Our responsibility rather is to share the gospel with those outside, but in complete dependence upon God, and in the expectation that the Holy Spirit will be at work through the gospel. If the Holy Spirit is working, especially in an extraordinary way, our evangelising will be eminently successful.

I wonder if it is possible for us today to hold these two things simultaneously in a Biblical equilibrium?

(c) Thirdly, there is a close and inseparable relationship between revival and prayer.

Elwyn was convinced that this was true, and essential, and Biblical. Nothing should take the place of prayer. If we wish to see God working powerfully again in Wales, Elwyn taught us, time and time again, that a central place must be given to prayer. But not to any kind of prayer. Our prayers, rather, should be honest, repentant, and from the heart, seeking God himself, his glory and his presence. Very often in such prayer the one who is praying experiences a liberty to plead before God on the basis of the promises of the Word. This was not mere theory to Elwyn. He looked himself for such prayers to be given to him or to others. And many times he received the privilege of praying in this manner.

Introduction

Let me give an example of an occasion when Elwyn prayed with the liberty of the Spirit. It was the first week of January 1948 and a Monday morning. A second retreat was being held at Dolgellau and on that morning, the last day of the retreat, a prayer meeting was held. Elwyn took part, and as he worshipped God and asked him for a blessing on the final sermon, he quoted the verse, Luke 11:13. He received liberty to plead the promise, asking the Father to give more of the Spirit to them according to that word. God answered his prayer even before he finished praying! Suddenly, as he prayed and pleaded, the Holy Spirit fell upon him, 'and filled me to such a degree with love for God,' he said, 'that I sat down sobbing and laughing at the same time.'[62] And later, after the sermon, the same thing occurred to all at the retreat. This was a foretaste of revival, a time of reality, an immense and extraordinary satisfaction and blessing – an example of the extraordinary work of the Spirit.

God is able to do this. And he is willing to do this also. But are we willing to give priority to prayer, as did Elwyn and his friends? This is the challenge to us today, rather than merely reading and speaking about revival. What about it?

Tributes and Reminiscences

J. Elwyn Davies (1925-2007)

A tribute that appeared in Y *Cylchgrawn Efengylaidd*, October 2007, and in Y *Ffordd Gadarn, Ysgrifau ar Lên a Chrefydd* by R. Geraint Gruffydd, papers on Welsh literature and religion, chosen and edited by E. Wyn James, Bryntirion Press, 2008.

The Reverend John Elwyn Davies (I shall refer to him as Elwyn from now on) died on Sunday afternoon, 29 July 2007, at Brynderwen resident home in Carmarthen, having celebrated his eighty-second birthday some two months earlier. He and his wife Mair had been married for forty-six years, and it is questionable whether there has ever been a couple more faithful to one another: Elwyn could have accomplished only a small part of all that he achieved without the unflinching support of Mair. The same faithfulness characterised the attitude of their children, together with their partners, towards their parents: Alun, Gwen, Hywel, Siân, Rhiain and Emyr. It was at the home of Rhiain and her husband Parry, in Carmarthen, that Elwyn and Mair were given a comfortable home and exemplary care during their last years together.

Elwyn was born at Terfyn, Rhostryfan, his father's family home, on 26 May 1925. His brother Gwylfa was born four years later; he died five months before Elwyn and is remembered with affection. The family lived in Caernarfon, however, for it was there that the father, Mr Robert George Davies, worked. I remember him well as a particularly kind-hearted person, as also was his wife (Mary Jarvis before her marriage), except that she was also a very shrewd lady with obvious organisational abilities. The boys received their education at Caernarfon, firstly at the Boys' Primary School and then at the Sir Hugh Owen Grammar School. They proved to be sufficiently able students to be accepted in due course by The University College of North Wales, Bangor: Elwyn in 1943, and Gwylfa in 1947. The family used to worship in Caernarfon, at Pendref Church initially and afterwards at Salem Congregational Chapel.

A Father in the Faith

By 1943, Elwyn had decided to become a minister with the Congregationalists, and he was received into Bala-Bangor College (the denomination's theological college at Bangor) with the intention of studying Theology, having first obtained an Arts degree. Gwylfa, on the other hand, had chosen the Law as his career. Elwyn's commitment and abilities were acknowledged from the start and before long he was appointed President of the SCM, the Students' Christian Movement, by far the most flourishing Christian society in Bangor at the time. As SCM President, he arranged after the war for the collection of food and clothes parcels to be sent to those who were experiencing extreme hardship amidst the ruins of Germany. According to his own testimony, as he was about this excellent work, he was convicted of spiritual pride, and that conviction eventually led to his evangelical conversion at a retreat during the Easter holidays of 1947. He graduated BA with a 2i degree in Philosophy that summer, and began his theological studies for a BD. During the summer he attended a conference for Christian students at Oslo, and was challenged and inspired by a young Christian girl, Ingeborg Zieseche, who was dying of tuberculosis but facing the future cheerfully and full of faith; he visited Germany also, meeting some of the people who had been helped by the parcel-collecting campaign.

When Elwyn returned to the College at Bangor in October 1947 his main interest was in evangelising. He arranged a retreat at Plas-y-nant, Capel Garmon, in January 1948 and many, including my wife and myself, embraced the Christian faith in its fullness at that retreat. However stumbling our walk may have been since, we could never thank Elwyn enough for placing us on the right path. He arranged a campaign at Bala during Easter 1948 which left a deep impression on the whole locality. Before the end of 1948 the *Cylchgrawn Efengylaidd* had been established, and a stall in the name of the *Cylchgrawn* was present on the field of the Dolgellau National Eisteddfod in 1949. As time passed, Elwyn drew to himself a number of very able committed co-workers: Emyr Roberts, T. Arthur Pritchard, Harold Jones, Emily Roberts, Gwilym Humphreys, Geraint Morgan and Herbert Evans, to name only a few of the more prominent.

By the academic year 1949-50 Elwyn was finding it more and more difficult to do justice to his academic work, partly because of the continuous call upon him to counsel those requiring help with spiritual matters. Before the end of the year he gave up his BD degree studies and decided to accept a call to the pastorate of Jerusalem Congregational Church, Blaenau Ffestiniog. This was not due to any fear of academic work – that great scholar, the late Professor J. E. Caerwyn Williams, spoke of 'the particular intellectual and spiritual abilities of the Rev. Elwyn Davies' – but to an awareness that could not be ignored of a higher calling. He was ordained and inducted as minister of Jerusalem at the end of September 1950 and remained there for five years, during which time his influence on the church and the locality was substantial. Six months after his ordination he married Mair Eluned Humphreys, a fellow-student at Bangor and a daughter of the Rev. James Humphreys, Rhosllannerchrugog, one of the leaders of the Presbyterian Church of Wales, and his wife Rachel. The joy and support that this marriage brought to Elwyn have already been mentioned, as have the births of his six children, which were similarly joyful occasions.

After five years in Jerusalem a new door opened for Elwyn and his family. In 1955 he was appointed Travelling Secretary to the Welsh IVF (the fellowship of evangelical Christian Unions in the university colleges), and he combined this post with the office of General Secretary of the Evangelical Movement of Wales, a responsibility which he shouldered for thirty-five years. By 1955 the Movement had been established, and the boundaries of its activities more or less defined. In June 1955 Elwyn and his family moved to Bala to live, helped by the gracious Pantyneuadd family (the first of many such families who were similarly hospitable). In less than a year Mair Jones from Llangennech had also moved to Bala to supervise the office work: her contribution to the growth of the Movement, together with that of Brenda Lewis who joined the staff in 1964, was priceless. The family, and the Movement office, remained at Bala for seven years, being housed in later years in rooms in the small country houses of Eryl Aran and Bryn-y-groes.

Then, in 1962, Elwyn and his family moved to Cwmafan near Port Talbot. Elwyn was invited to become the part-time minister of Seion Congregational Church, Cwmafan, and the family lived in the church manse before moving to Blaen-y-wawr, Bridgend, not far from the Movement's new headquarters at Bryntirion, Bridgend. Accompanying this move he received a call to be the part-time pastor of Free School Court Church, Bridgend, where he stayed for eleven years. He left a deep impression on all the congregations where he ministered: in Cwmafan and Bridgend (and, for a short period, in Pontarddulais also).

A Father in the Faith

His main responsibility during these years, however, was the oversight of the growth of the Evangelical Movement, with the help of many fellow-ministers and of many able and committed staff workers. Under his leadership the *seiat* meetings, the evangelistic campaigns, the conferences, the camps, the publications and the bookshops, flourished. In 1985 the Evangelical Theological College of Wales was established and for many years Elwyn was the President of the College. The evangelical message, over the years, became known and was heard throughout the country, although the reaction to it was not at all commensurate with Elwyn's desire.

He played his part also in the wider evangelical world, with the ready encouragement and support of Dr Martyn Lloyd-Jones, a faithful friend for many years. For three years (1969-72) Elwyn was President of the British Evangelical Council – I remember Canon Michael Green inquiring warmly after him when visiting Aberystwyth – and he and Mair experienced times of blessing ministering in Patagonia, in Australia (twice) and in the United States. From one point of view the Movement represented the powerful reaction against liberal theology that was one aspect of Protestant church life in the West from the end of the First World War onwards, but together with this it combined a consistent emphasis on the experiential aspect of the Christian message and life: Calvinistic Methodism indeed! I remember the most prominent advocate of this reaction in Wales, Professor J. E. Daniel, questioning me in detail as to what had occurred at Bangor under Elwyn's leadership at the end of 1947 and beginning of 1948, and rejoicing greatly on hearing the news. Clearly he held Elwyn in great regard.

From a human standpoint it may be said with confidence that the Evangelical Movement was predominantly Elwyn's creation, and it cannot be said for very many religious leaders that their vision became incorporated in a movement that continued to proclaim their message long after their own period. Yet my own impression over the years has been that Elwyn was not particularly enamoured of administration, committee meetings and politics (in the ecclesiastical sense). I doubt whether he took much delight in the discussions on the possible restructuring of the Movement during the 1970s and 1980s, though he presided over the changes wisely and graciously. Elwyn's greatest delight always was meditating upon the message of the Bible – particularly that of his favourite Gospel of John – and then sharing the fruit of his meditations to as many people as wished to hear him. Very often when listening to Elwyn, the hearers would be aware that he was heavily under the influence of the Holy Spirit. Indeed, as with Dr Martyn Lloyd-Jones, he was reluctant to climb into a pulpit without a sense of that unction upon his own spirit. I remember praising a preacher at the Welsh Conference of the Movement on one occasion, and he agreed that it was as good a sermon as might be had, 'without the unction'! Another aspect of the same attitude was his firm belief that nothing but another revival could restore Wales spiritually.

Elwyn and Mair moved to Heulwen, Pen-y-cae, Port Talbot in 1992 and from there to Ar-y-bryn, Parc Penllwyn, Carmarthen in 1997. As already mentioned, this was the home of their daughter Rhiain and her husband Parry, who looked after them – in an exemplary manner – from then onwards. Two years earlier, through a tragic accident, Rhiain and Parry had lost their young son, Dafydd Elwyn, and this was a crushing blow to Elwyn and Mair, as well as to Rhiain and Parry and their two daughters. They suffered other losses as time went by. Dr Martyn Lloyd-Jones, Elwyn's mentor in many respects, died in 1981, and his dear friend, Emyr Roberts in 1988; so also another great friend, T. Arthur Pritchard, in 1997. A year previously, Elwyn had learnt from the consultant at Morriston Hospital, Dr Richard Weiser, that he was suffering from Parkinson's Disease, but that everything would be done to manage the symptoms. (Dr Weiser testified to Mair after Elwyn's death that his peaceful spirit and his courage in facing his illness had made a permanent impression upon him.)

Yet these last years were not without their highlights in Elwyn's history. His addresses to the Evangelical Movement's Welsh Conference in 1996, 'O! Ryfedd Ras,'[63] were published in 1998: a particularly valuable publication. And in 2001 Elwyn and Mair celebrated their golden wedding. Throughout this period, however, Mair was suffering increasingly from rheumatism, resulting in a series of operations. Yet, I found them both always cheerful and joyful, and although Elwyn suffered a fall in 2003 which also required corrective surgery, and though his disease affected the clarity of his mind at times, yet their son Hywel could testify that he remained 'the same old Elwyn' to the end. He was a faithful witness to his Lord for over sixty years after the momentous dealings between the two in Easter 1947, and there are many hundreds in Wales who have reason to be thankful to God for Elwyn, and for Mair.

R. Geraint Gruffydd

Early memories

Elwyn played an important part in my life from my youth, when we used to live in adjacent streets in Caernarfon.

I remember my mother saying often that she remembered Elwyn, Gwylfa (his brother – who was my age) and myself sitting on the same seat of a bus travelling from Caernarfon to Rhostryfan. They were with their parents on their way to visit their grandmother, and I was with my parents on the way to meet friends at Rhostryfan. The picture of the three of us fitting on the one bus seat had made an impression on my mother, and she had thought, 'I wonder what will become of the three of them when they grow up?' And, thankfully, the three of us, by the grace of God, came to know the Lord Jesus Christ.

We attended the same school, the County School as it was then called, though Elwyn was three years older than myself. On one occasion Elwyn arranged for fifteen of us, younger children, boys and girls, to cycle from Caernarfon to Trefor, a journey of about fifteen miles, after school. We met on the *Maes*[64] at four o'clock and set out for Trefor. Elwyn advised us not to race but to keep on cycling at a steady pace – advice that Elwyn adhered to throughout his life, keeping on and persevering, as the Word emphasises. After reaching Trefor, we left our bikes at the *Aelwyd*,[65] climbed over two of the Eifl mountains to Llanaelhaearn, and then walked the two miles back to Trefor. Finally, a cycle back home; altogether quite an achievement after a day's work at school.

Elwyn loved to play football and was a member of the school's first team for many years. A friend, who was in the sixth form with him, told me lately that Elwyn had arranged a prayer meeting at five o'clock in a chapel vestry on a Saturday night, and that about twelve to fifteen of them from the school were at the meeting. Afterwards most of them went together to the 'pictures', that is, the cinema.

A Father in the Faith

If there were any inter-church meetings in the town, the three of us, Elwyn, Gwylfa and myself, together with about two others, would always be there.

I met Elwyn again at the Christian Union at Bangor University College: Elwyn at the University and myself at St Mary's College (a college for women student-teachers). We were talking one day and he said to me, 'Rina, I don't think that you are a Christian.' That Elwyn, of all people, should say such a thing! He knew me so well, knew that I was a good girl who attended chapel three times a Sunday and desired to live an upright life! He asked me, 'Do you believe in the Lord Jesus Christ?' 'Yes,' I said, in all honesty and with no doubt. He then asked a second time, 'Do you believe in the LORD Jesus Christ?' Why ask a second time? 'Yes,' I said again. Then he asked, 'Is Jesus Christ the Lord – the Lord – of your life, or is it you yourself?'

I began to feel uncomfortable and to rebel inwardly. I have the right to rule my own life, I thought, and I am the one to decide what I want to do. It is all very well to go to chapel on Sundays and to learn of Jesus Christ, but I wished to live an independent life, apart from him. I reasoned with myself: If I say that I believe in the Lord Jesus Christ, and that he is Lord, then he must become Lord over every part of my life. That night I yielded my life to the Lord Jesus, and I thank God that Elwyn confronted me with the fact of his Lordship.

I have experienced over the sixty years since that time that to work out the Lordship of Christ in every part of my life, and to bend to his will, is the essence of the Christian life.

Rina Macdonald

A gimpse of Caernarfon days

The first time I saw Elwyn was in the County School, Caernarfon (afterwards the Grammar School, and now Ysgol Syr Hugh Owen). He was about three years older than me so we did not know one another well. However, I remember how we were allowed to listen on occasions to those of Elwyn's age debating current issues, and to hear how they considered the various contributions, for and against. The way in which Elwyn dealt with issues, and presented his argument, impressed me at the time. He would never get worked up or try to gain a point in any way, but only delivered his viewpoint clearly and deliberately.

He never forgot Caernarfon town, or the school. He wrote in my copy of his book, *Striving Together*, when I asked him for his signature in August 1984: 'With fond memories of the old town and school.' I remember that the last time he came to Caernarfon was when he stayed with Hywel some years ago. He was able to visit his cousin and to reminisce about old times.

Apart from his books and addresses at the Conference, we knew that his great strength lay in his personal work. In September 1949 I experienced this for the first time. Elwyn was leading a Movement campaign in Caernarfon, and the Rev. Emyr Roberts was preaching. I had an experience of the Lord that night, and was led to pray. Elwyn walked with me to the bus that would take me home. He had an attractive personality but what I remember is that he did not draw attention to himself but directed attention to the Lord. His last sentence to me was, 'Remember to ask the Lord for a verse on which to establish your experience.' This I did, and the Lord graciously answered my prayer the next morning.

After I had written a letter to express my joy and sent it to him, he called me on the phone at work – his home, Bryn Eryr, was across the road to the office at that time. He arranged for us to meet as he wished to present me to a friend of his, Celt Hughes, who was in Eryri

Hospital, Caernarfon. By this time, Celt could not move hand or foot, or do anything for himself. He also could not speak but, as you got to know him, you could discern what he wished to say as he articulated the beginnings of words.

Elwyn would accompany Celt outside for a walk in his wheelchair, and we would hold prayer-meetings on a stretch of grass near the hospital. We were fortunate in the weather from the September to the middle of October. I heard Elwyn describe how Arthur Pritchard had been given a vision of flames passing through Wales. As I look back, Elwyn's faith in the work that would be accomplished in Wales was very evident. I feel that this was the beginning of the Movement.

Another event in Caernarfon was the April Campaign of 1950, with Elwyn preaching in the square on Saturday night. The unction of the Holy Spirit was undoubtedly upon him. A twenty-year-old girl came to me afterwards saying that she had never heard anything like it; she had been greatly blessed. That young girl died of meningitis some two years afterwards, and I was so thankful that she had been brought to the faith during the Campaign.

Another area that showed Elwyn's concern for Caernarfon was his request to Dennis Jenkins (when the latter was ministering at Deiniolen) to establish an evangelical *seiat* in the town. I remember being with the two of them as they discussed the matter, and being impressed at Elwyn's longing for fellowship based upon the Word.

Of course, we cannot speak of Elwyn without thinking of Mair. I once travelled with her from Llanymawddwy, when she was at Brynuchaf,[66] and I had been staying with Emily and Wena.[67] Elwyn and Mair were about to marry at that time. The bus arrived on the *Maes* at Caernarfon. I can still see Elwyn running from the Post Office towards the bus, and the two of them shaking hands. Not embracing – there was nothing superficial and public in their relationship, but a deep, warm mutual understanding. The ideal marriage, as we know.

As I think of Elwyn's faithfulness and service to the Lord, I believe that I cannot say more than to repeat the title of one of his books, '*O! Ryfedd Ras*'.

Joan Hughes

A man of vision

From *The Evangelical Magazine*, June/July 1990

It was in the autumn of 1947 that I first made Elwyn's acquaintance. We met to draw up a programme for a Christian weekend conference or 'retreat' to be held at Dolgellau in the New Year. Little did we realise then what the Lord had in store for us, but we both know now that what happened at Dolgellau forged a close bond of friendship between us.

Those who came to that retreat experienced the presence of the Holy Spirit in our midst in a remarkable way, and many were brought to faith in Jesus Christ during and after it. We were also given an assurance that we would see a new work of God's grace becoming more and more evident in our land.

It was the vision for this that made Elwyn the man that he is. His life-work was inspired and directed by an intense desire to see its fulfilment and to contribute towards it in every possible way. Nothing less could have enabled him to leave the pastoral ministry so close to his heart and undertake a wider ministry as EMW General Secretary.

His strength of character, determination and perseverance, combined with his warmth and compassionate personality, are evidence that God had prepared him for such a ministry. A man of deep faith and convictions, he is patient and persuasive in sharing his vision with others, yet readily acknowledges that the will of God is often made known through the prayerful deliberations of God's people. To know the warmth and integrity of his friendship has been a privilege shared by many throughout these years. In the materialistic climate of our day he has been a valiant defender of the faith and a man with a deep concern for souls.

We thank God for one of whom it can be said that he was 'not disobedient unto the heavenly vision'. The timing of his retirement this year, though richly deserved, was determined primarily by his faithfulness to marital and family responsibilities. We respect him all the more for this, and pray that by the grace of God he will yet be enabled to see a greater fulfilment of that vision for His work to prosper in our land.

T. Arthur Pritchard

A campaign in Trefor

When I heard of the death of the Rev. J. Elwyn Davies on Sunday, 29 July, I experienced a great longing and yearning for the years at the end of the 1940s and the beginning of the 1950s when Emyr Roberts, my husband, was a young minister in the village of Trevor in Arfon. It was a hard time, and Emyr and his co-workers realised that many of the young people, after the horrors of the war and the dreadful losses, were choosing not to return to the chapels.

Trefor and its surroundings was a locality that was economically dependent on the granite quarry and, compared to later periods, these years were relatively destitute and needy. Gosen Chapel (Calvinistic Methodist) had for some years been without a pastor, and Emyr felt the need to quicken the church and to attempt to motivate the youngsters of his pastorate. This was when Elwyn was a student at the Congregational College in Bangor (Bala-Bangor as it was called). The Student Christian Movement was active in the college, and Elwyn was convinced that the gospel had to be taken to the people. Many of the students arranged evangelistic campaigns with ministers who were eager to obtain their help in order to share and witness to the gospel, and a week of meetings was arranged for Trefor, with some of the visitors staying at local homes. A prayer meeting for the team was held every morning, and some went to speak and witness to those in the quarry during their dinner hour. A public meeting was then held every night to proclaim the good news, and one or two of the young people – who had experienced forgiveness and the reality of faith in Jesus Christ as Saviour – gave testimony to their faith, their experience and their joy.

My own experience at the time was of inadequacy, and I laboured hard to overcome my selfishness and pride, my lack of love and concern for my neighbours. That week became a great blessing for Emyr and myself and for a number of Trefor people. We were given an assurance of God's great gift in Christ and of his death on our behalf on the cross to reconcile us to God. Elwyn was the means of leading me to accept that great gift, without anything required on my part, and to realise that Christ was my Friend. The Bible became a new book to me, and the great hymns expressed real experiences. For example:

Mi dafla' 'maich oddi ar fy ngwar
wrth deimlo dwyfol loes;
euogrwydd fel mynyddoedd byd
dry'n ganu wrth dy groes.[68]

I throw my burden off my back
on sensing divine pain;
a weight of guilt like the world's
                                    mountains
turns to singing at your cross.

How grateful I am for Elwyn and for his willingness to serve his Lord and to give so much to so many of us through his ministry over the years. The work begun over fifty years ago continues, and for two generations new pastors have laboured in the fields. I give thanks for the faithful witnesses who work and pray diligently for revival to visit us again in our day.

Grace Roberts

A father in the Faith

From *The Evangelical Magazine*, November/December 2007

J. Elwyn Davies became the minister of our church, Jerusalem, Blaenau Ffestiniog, in 1950. In college, he was friendly with my uncle and I called him by his first name, but when he became our minister I had strict orders from my Nain (Gran) to address him always as 'Mr Davies'.

He began a discipleship class to prepare young people for membership of our church. My friend Nerys (now Cooper) attended the first year of classes. One day she said to me, 'I've become a Christian.' I was flabbergasted. I decided there and then that I would not follow suit. I was as good as I wanted to be!

Six of us attended the discipleship class the following year. The relevance of the death of Christ was explained to us. That was the first time I'd ever heard that Jesus Christ was of real, personal relevance to anybody, other than ministers. In his quiet earnest way, with a smile on his face, Mr Davies made clear to us our need to repent and accept Christ as our personal Saviour. He explained that there was no point in becoming a member of the church without really knowing and trusting the Lord Jesus Christ. Nevertheless, in my heart I was quite defiant. But, during one restless night, a few month's later, I came to a moment of truth. In the darkness I prayed that I might not be physically or spiritually blind. On my way home from school that day I went to see Mr Davies at his home. Yes, of course he would see me. He serenely took time to explain the gospel and to pray with me. From that day I knew I was a Christian. Several of my friends made a profession of faith at that time and a weekly Scripture Union was arranged.

Mr Davies preached at our wedding. We have always enjoyed fellowship with him and Mrs Davies. Through the years, as he did with others, he always gave us his full attention, passing on wise counsel and warm encouragements. He was a spiritual man, warm-hearted, kind, a true father in the faith – and I always called him Mr Davies!

Rhiain Lewis

A wise pastor

Affection and seriousness were Elwyn's main characteristics. He approached the work of preaching as an awesome work. He never ascended a pulpit carelessly or complacently, and at a prayer meeting he would pray with all seriousness. We were always aware that he was seeking God's presence.

For him, to evangelise was to do God's work, and to build up believers in the faith was God's work also. This is why he would set aside much time for speaking to those who were searching for the truth. And this also is why he would arrange a series of meetings to instruct recent converts in the faith. Everyone was aware that their spiritual health was of supreme importance to him. His pastoral care was very great.

He would aim to channel the enthusiasm of new converts to effective service and to witness by word and deed to the new grace that had come into their lives. It is as a result of his encouragement that many a testimony or article by young converts were found in the early issues of the *Cylchgrawn Efengylaidd*.

Elwyn always reminded us to be careful never to give any avoidable offence that could hinder the progress of the gospel. One example of this arose in the arrangements for our weddings. He would encourage young couples to honour their minister – even though that minister, perhaps, might not be of an evangelical persuasion – by asking him to take the wedding service. And then Elwyn himself would be willing to be the best man and therefore be able to steer the proceedings so that the speeches would not be embarrassing or inappropriate. In so many situations, his advice was wise and practical.

His burden for revival was great – a direct result of his own extensive experience of the Holy Spirit in his personal life and in his ministry.

A Father in the Faith

I cannot think of a more appropriate verse to reflect the secret of his life than that which was printed on a card in each copy of an early issue of the *Cylchgrawn Efengylaidd*:

N'ad fod gennyf ond d'ogoniant
Pur, sancteiddiol, yma a thraw,
Yn union nod o flaen fy amrant,
Pa beth bynnag wnêl fy llaw;
Treulio mywyd,
F'unig fywyd, er dy glod.[69]

Let it only be your glory –
Pure and sacred – at all times,
That shall be the one goal before me,
Whatever my hand finds to do,
Living my life,
My only life, for your glory.

Geraint Morgan

Maintaining a vision

From *Y Cylchgrawn Efengylaidd*, October 2007.
The Rev. Dr Noel Gibbard is the author of *The First Fifty Years: A History of the Evangelical Movement of Wales 1948-98*, Bryntirion Press, 2002

I am grateful for this opportunity of writing something on Elwyn. Apart from the fact that he was a person worth knowing, he was of great help to me on many occasions at important times in my life. He enriched me in many ways and I am indebted to him. That also is the testimony of Helen, my wife.

I knew of the Rev. J. Elwyn Davies before going to college at Bangor. I knew that he was the editor of the *Cylchgrawn Efengylaidd* and I used to receive copies of that magazine whilst a pupil at Gwendraeth Grammar School. In one of the early issues I read an article by Mair Humphreys, Rhosllannerchrugog, 'Dr Jekyll and Mr Hyde', in which she described the duality in her life before coming to faith in Jesus Christ. This was the kind of discussion that was occurring in school also at that time.

By the time I reached college, Elwyn Davies and Mair Humphreys had recently married and had settled at 'Bronllwyn', Blaenau Ffestiniog, where Elwyn was the minister of Jerusalem Congregational Chapel. It was there, in their home, that I met the two of them for the first time. I had been preaching at Bryn Bowydd, and went to visit them after the evening service. It was good to hear of the spiritual quickening that had begun in 1947, and of their experiences while settling in at Blaenau. Many of the young people had come to faith in the Saviour very soon after their arrival, and on a further visit to Blaenau, to preach at Jerusalem, I saw some of them coming to look for 'Mr Davies'. When visiting Jerusalem it was a precious experience to be at the prayer meeting before the service in the company of Herbert Evans, full of the new wine, and William Roberts and Mrs Jones, two mature believers.

I had another connection with Elwyn in that, at the college, I lodged with his brother, Gwylfa. Elwyn would come to visit Bangor and, after a few years at Blaenau, he came more regularly, having been appointed Travelling Secretary for the Inter-Varsity Fellowship. I would meet with him to discuss the activities at Bangor, and my previous knowledge of him would be amply confirmed. I experienced again his firm tenderness and his spiritual discernment. He would advise on the details of arrangements, on personal experiences, or on the implications of faith in the Saviour. It was he who suggested to me, as he did to others, no doubt, that as a student I should face up to my financial responsibility towards the work of the Lord in Wales.

Detailed exposition

I would also attend conferences where Elwyn was leading or speaking. He concentrated particularly on two themes: those found in John, chapter 15, and the Lord's Prayer, from Matthew 6:5-15. Time meant nothing to Elwyn once he began to preach. I heard him preaching for an hour often, and sometimes for an hour and a half, but however long the journey Elwyn would always reach the destination. His sermons were characterised by detailed exposition. He would normally deal with a paragraph, such as the one containing the Lord's Prayer, but any paragraph is part of a chapter, therefore the context had to be understood in detail. What was the background? What was the theme? At times, when preaching, Elwyn liked to use illustrations from domestic life. He once, for example, was speaking of the love of God for his people. He referred to the careful, diligent mother, preparing a meal. Naturally she was concentrating on that particular meal, but in her mind was the provision for the rest of the day, and indeed for the day after. And the differing needs of each one of the family would also be in her thoughts. So also with God. It is he who ordains, and in doing so the particular needs of each one of his children is known to him, and each one is precious in his sight.

Memories

I must speak of the 'van'. Or rather, not so much of the van, but of Elwyn's driving of the van. I remember travelling often with him and it was always clear that his target was to arrive as soon as possible, though he was also a careful driver. During this period it was a joy to visit the family after they had moved to Bala, firstly in the town and then at Eryl Aran. The story of how they bought Eryl Aran, while at the same time their eye was on another mansion, over the garden hedge, was wonderful. And soon the latter, Bryn-y-groes, became the headquarters of the Evangelical Movement of Wales.

Helen and I were very glad to have him present at our wedding in Calfaria, Aberdare. This chapel was a significant place both for him and for Helen. It was there that Helen was raised, and Elwyn had preached there ten years previously. He had taken the place of his friend, Celt Hughes, who was in poor health. Their friendship was like that of David and Jonathan. Celt had visited Calfaria once, before Elwyn's visit, on a Sunday that had included a children's service. Helen remembers standing beside Celt in the pulpit, waiting to take her part in the service. Calfaria was to extend a call to Celt, and Helen's father was one of the company from the chapel who travelled to Caernarfon to visit him in the hospital. Celt died before the date set for his ordination service.

Elwyn failed to come to my own ordination services in Pen-y-wern, Dowlais, but he was present at my induction service at Berea, Bynea, and he preached together with Dr Tudur Jones. This was truly a feast. It was also another significant day, apart from being an induction service. It was the day that Principal Gwilym Bowyer died. He had been Principal when I and my brothers, Ithel and Headley, were at Bala-Bangor College, and was Headley's father-in-law. Elwyn preached on the first part of John's Gospel, chapter 14.

A wise counsellor
Times arise in life when important decisions have to be made, and it is highly beneficial at such times to have someone to advise you. There were many occasions when Elwyn was my adviser, and the following are some examples. After some years at Bynea I received an invitation to lecture at a particular college. My own natural response was to accept the invitation, and yet there was some uncertainty in my heart. I called Elwyn and arranged to meet him. At that time, the *Cylchgrawn* was printed at Briton Ferry and Elwyn asked me to meet him there. After seeing the printer, Elwyn and I walked together for some time. Elwyn thought of all the possibilities, and believed quite firmly that I should not accept the invitation. I had peace of mind after this, and within a year, more or less, I was offered a lecturing post at Barry Bible College.

Elwyn believed that it was vital for ministers to meet together for prayer and study. There was a constant need for consistent evangelical preaching, and one stimulus for this was the arranging of meetings for fellowship. There was no ministers' fraternal in the Merthyr area when I went to Dowlais. Elwyn knew this and came over to our home to discuss the possibilities. The two of us visited the Rev. Eurfyl Jones in Trecynon, Aberdare, and we agreed to begin an English fraternal. Aberdare was the venue for some time and we then transferred to Pontypridd where more ministers were able to gather with us.

Elwyn did everything within his power to support the Welsh-speaking witness in Wales: through personal conversation, through the *Cylchgrawn*, by evangelising, and by encouraging the Welsh-speaking evangelical causes. He was saddened at the lack of a Welsh witness in the Bridgend/Cardiff region. Occasional meetings were arranged at Bryntirion, Bridgend, with Elwyn and myself preaching. This was not satisfactory but Elwyn urged perseverance. Wyn James, Gwylfa (Elwyn's brother), and I met to consider the options. As a result, we began to meet in Cardiff, firstly in a home, and then in Tŷ'r Cymry.[70] Unfortunately we missed Elwyn's company for a time, while he and Mair were in Australia. On his return he preached to us, taking the first part of Colossians 3 as his text.

'Still waiting'

When I started to write the history of the Evangelical Movement, it was impossible to begin without consulting the original source, or rather, the original sources, Elwyn and Mair. For about a year and half I had the privilege of visiting them in their home in Carmarthen. Elwyn would get caught up in the story and sometimes Mair would have to break in and say, 'No, Elwyn, that wasn't how it happened.' The history was described in detail and a few themes discussed – revival in particular. At one point Elwyn described his relationship with Dr Martyn Lloyd-Jones, and the emphasis on revival. With reference to revival Elwyn said, with tears on his cheeks, 'I've been spoilt for anything else.' His response was the same during his last illness at the home in Llangunnor. When he mentioned revival, I said to him, 'You're still waiting,' and his reply, in a weak but determined voice, was, 'Yes, still waiting.' It is impossible to forget the dimension of revival when remembering Elwyn Davies.

A connecting link

He was not one to compromise, but was always ready to consolidate. I like to think of Elwyn as a connecting link. He ensured the continuance of evangelical witness by means of a periodical. Although the *Efengylydd*[71] and the *Cylchgrawn Efengylaidd* were very different magazines, in the essentials they were one. Some of the contributors to the *Efengylydd* wrote for the *Cylchgrawn*, Nantlais and Owen Thomas, Llantrisant, for example. Some time ago, Elwyn gave me the personal Bible of R. B. Jones, Porth, in order to present it to the college in Bryntirion. He had received it from David Evans, Bridgend, another – together with R. B. Jones – of the *Efengylydd* company, and Elwyn was one of his successors at the 'Mission' in Bridgend. There was a theological difference between the two magazines in that the *Cylchgrawn* represented a more Calvinistic tradition than the *Efengylydd*. Theological differences were evident within the Evangelical Movement also, but Elwyn was always one of the first to ensure that ministers and other leaders were not estranged from one another. The unity of the saints was important to him, as was seen in his work in Wales, in his involvement with the British Evangelical Council, and in his journey to Australia to encourage evangelical unity.

Elwyn was foremost also in the discussions between Barry Bible College and the Evangelical Movement for forming an evangelical college. This was eventually achieved in 1985, safeguarding the continuity of evangelical witness. He was the President of the Evangelical Theological College of Wales for many years. One of his hopes was of seeing Welsh-medium tuition in the College. The Welsh-speaking witness was a great burden upon him, as we have seen. He never wearied of emphasising the Welsh roots of the Evangelical Movement. Yet, no-one worked harder than he to encourage the English-speaking side of the work, thus ensuring that the two emphases were but aspects of the same activity.

Noel Gibbard

Thankful memories

It is a great pleasure to respond to the invitation to remember the ministry of the Rev. Elwyn Davies. I first came in contact with him as a student at University College, Bangor, when he was Travelling Secretary for the IVF (the Inter-Varsity Fellowship), the UCCF by now. We looked forward to his visits, which were at least once a term, and we greatly appreciated his warm, Biblical preaching. At that time the Travelling Secretary was responsible for the Christian Unions in all the colleges of the University of Wales – Cardiff, Swansea, Aberystwyth and Bangor (the Christian Union at Lampeter was formed later, I believe), but Elwyn Davies would not hide the fact that he very much enjoyed returning to Bangor. After all, that was where he himself had been a diligent student, and it was at an SCM retreat at Plas-y-nant, between Caernarfon and Beddgelert, that God came down in evident blessing and saved a number of Welsh men and women who were to be the enthusiastic instruments in God's hand for establishing the Evangelical Movement.

One of the highlights of the Christian Union at Bangor during my period there (1958-64) was the annual Retreat held at Plas-y-nant a few days before the beginning of the Easter term. Often it would have been snowing and the views of the neighbouring mountains and of Llyn Cwellyn were spectacular. The first evening involved an open *seiat*. This was my first experience of an experience meeting, and although it was not always a comfortable business to contribute honestly and positively, yet, under the firm but gentle leadership of Elwyn Davies, it was always a very valuable and edifying time. As might be expected, there were sessions set aside for prayer, for discussion and for studying the Word, and after two whole days during which we had listened to addresses by Elwyn Davies on a key portion of the Word, Romans 5-8, or John 15, or, at another time, Luke 11 (the Lord's Prayer), we were quickened spiritually and well prepared to be more worthy witnesses to Jesus.

In addition, Elwyn Davies's visits would be greatly anticipated by those with particular difficulties, those, for example, who were studying Theology or Biblical Studies. Most of the lectures in those subjects at that time were very liberal. The evangelical standpoint was completely disregarded, and evangelical Christians had to discover for themselves how to understand and expound difficult areas of the Bible, such as the opening chapters of Genesis, the authorship of the Pentateuch, the unity of the prophecy of Isaiah, or the sources of the Synoptic Gospels. (How different it is now with the great range of excellent evangelical publications available in our Christian shops or on the Internet.) And who better, at the end of the 50s and the beginning of the 60s, to provide guidance than Elwyn Davies who had had to face these questions himself and had thought deeply over them and was able to point us in the right direction. Others had personal problems which they wished to discuss. He had the rare gift of listening and thinking before responding. You felt that he understood you and that he was giving his full attention to your problem.

Those are some of the impressions that have remained with me since college days. I consider myself and my contemporaries privileged to have had such a person as a role model at such a crucial time in our lives. His paternal nature and warm voice soon gained our affection and earned our respect at the same time. This admiration and appreciation of him remained throughout the years. It was not only as a student but also in later years, on many occasions, when he himself was carrying heavy burdens as the General Secretary of the Evangelical Movement, I benefited greatly by sharing problems with him.

I end my comments with a few verses from the Letter to the Hebrews, chapter 13:7-8: 'Remember them which have the rule over you, who have spoken unto you the word of God: whose faith follow, considering the end of their conversation. Jesus Christ the same yesterday, and today, and for ever.' Certainly, Elwyn Davies was one of these.

Ioan Davies

IVF Travelling Secretary

From *The Evangelical Magazine*, November/December 2007. One of the books written by Geraint Fielder is *Excuse Me, Mr Davies – Hallelujah: Evangelistic Student Witness in Wales, 1923-1983* (Bryntirion Press, 1983). The book describes the contributions of Elwyn Davies and others to the Christian witness in the colleges of Wales, and he is the 'Mr Davies' of the title.

Elwyn Davies was by far the greatest single influence on my Christian life as a student. Many of my contemporaries would say the same. He had been converted when a student at Bangor in 1947, and his testimony the following Sunday led to the conversion of fellow student Mair Humphreys, later his wife and sterling supporter in the work.

The absorbing events of the years 1947-9 in Bangor and beyond are crucial for an understanding of the way evangelical life developed in Wales for a generation. During his years as Inter-Varsity Fellowship Travelling Secretary in Wales (1955-62) three characteristics stand out for me.

First, he established the pattern of giving the main ministry at each annual Christian Union conference or 'retreat'. This helped to set the tone throughout the CUs, and the theme he dealt with would often emerge as a prominent note in the life of the CUs – a testimony to the way God spoke through those messages.

Second, at the heart of his gift for cultivating the spiritual life was the *seiat*. Everyone was encouraged to share his present Christian experience, whether encouraging or otherwise. This was a most effective way of ensuring that everyone present measured their own progress, not merely by the amount of teaching understood and accepted, but also by the extent to which this was affecting one's life and character.

Third, what Elwyn's ministry awakened most in the hearts of students in that era was a hunger for revival. Students often said that this was the most valuable perspective they gained from his ministry. His teaching about the glory of God moulded our own thinking about evangelism and revival, and we made it our own.

It was with some measure of awe but also a sense of honour that I succeeded him as travelling secretary.

Geraint Fielder

EMW General Secretary

From *The Evangelical Magazine,* June/July 1990, on the occasion of Elwyn Davies's retirement from the work of General Secretary of the Evangelical Movement of Wales.

You mention Shakespeare and think of drama; or Handel and your mind turns to music; mention J. Elwyn Davies, and you cannot avoid thinking of the Evangelical Movement of Wales. The work and the man are indistinguishable. That this is so is due not only to the fact of history but also to his complete and utter commitment to the Movement's work.

Historically, he was there at the beginning. In 1948 his name appears on the first issue of *Y Cylchgrawn Efengylaidd* (The Welsh Evangelical Magazine) as *Ysg. Gohebol* (the Correspondence Secretary). To readers of the *Evangelical Magazine* those beginnings may be shrouded in the mists of Celtic mystery; but to us who were privileged to be involved they were days of a new clarity in our perception of the eternal gospel, of the glowing light of the Holy Spirit, and of a burning warmth of heart towards our Lord and Saviour. There was no EMW then – just *Ffrindiau'r Cylchgrawn* (Friends of the Magazine). Two factors united us: our common experience of God's grace, and God's providential gift of a common language which we spoke and loved. Our vision was towards Welsh-speaking people who were strangers to the gospel and the Saviour it proclaimed.

This is not the time to trace the history of the Movement, but merely to acknowledge the place of Elwyn under God in that history. He has been there at every stage: at the purchase of Eryl Aran, Bala – a crucial development – and then of Bryn-y-groes; at the removal of the office to Port Talbot in 1962, when he and his family were prepared to be uprooted from their beloved north Wales; at the remarkable provision of Bryntirion in 1970; and in the Movement's developing spheres of ministry over the years.

A Father in the Faith

Among the qualities that have equipped him for his task one would note the visionary dimension – he dreams dreams, and by God's grace has seen some of them come to fruition; tenacity of purpose, tempered by respect for the opinion of others – it has been a story of bringing together of brethren to one mind and purpose; the methodical discipline of a trained mind; and the heart of a shepherd of God's people. His work has involved him in pastoring the staff of the Movement. He has advised and cared for many a pastor through difficult times. He has been mediator and counsellor in broken relationships. To many he has been a man of God, to others their father in Christ.

Gareth H. Davies

Remembering Elwyn

I first met Elwyn after going to Bangor to study Theology. As a member with the Congregationalists, I was a student at Bala-Bangor College. A few years previously Elwyn, who was also a Congregationalist, had studied at the same College, so that there was common ground between us from our first acquaintance.

Elwyn would visit Bangor regularly in his role as Travelling Secretary for the Christian Unions. He was an easy person to get to know and we had many interesting conversations discussing issues such as the spiritual needs of students, the denominations, and the state of Wales as a nation. He was optimistic that the situation could be improved. He believed passionately in the need for revival, and he emphasised the importance of remaining true to the Scriptures and continuing in prayer in order to obtain it. He was faithful and hard-working as a Travelling Secretary and many former students still mention the help and support that they received from him.

It was at one of the Christian Union meetings in Bangor that I first met my wife, Ceinwen. As she was the sister of Mair, Elwyn's wife, my connections with Elwyn and Mair were bound to strengthen as Ceinwen and I continued our courtship. I received a warm welcome at all times at their home, and I am very thankful for their kindness. I had the opportunity to get to know Elwyn in his own home and we enjoyed talking and sharing together. Though essentially a serious and earnest man, a healthy humour was always close to the surface.

Elwyn loved to expound the Scriptures. He was a master at leading a retreat. I still remember a series of edifying addresses that he gave at Plas-y-nant (nearly fifty years ago) as he took three sessions to explain 1 Corinthians 1:30-31: 'But of him are ye in Christ Jesus, who of God is made unto us wisdom, and righteousness, and sanctification, and redemption: That according as it is written, He that glorieth, let him glory in the Lord.' During the retreats he also had opportunity to enjoy fellowship with individuals and small groups.

When my time came to begin work in the ministry at Port Talbot, Elwyn and the family had already moved to Cwmafan, and Elwyn was pastoring Seion Chapel. As we lived so close to one another, and the Movement's office was also at Port Talbot, we had many profitable conversations, and he was always willing to offer advice and was supportive of my work in the church.

During this period the work of the Movement increased and Elwyn was at the forefront of the expansion of the Welsh work and, particularly, that on the English side. Our close connections continued after we moved to Cardiff, though we saw less of each other. He and Mair were always interested in our family, and we would meet on special family occasions in our home and at Carmarthen. We value the privilege of having known him for over fifty years.

Hefin Elias

A wise counsellor and prophetic preacher

As a family we must have become known to Elwyn soon after he moved with his family to Bala in 1955. At that time we lived at Tyn-y-bont which is about four miles up Cwm Tryweryn from Bala. We worshipped at Tyn-y-bont Congregational Chapel, and Elwyn would often preach there. I must confess that my heart would sink when I heard his name being announced as the preacher for the following Sunday. I knew that we would have a lengthy sermon and that we would have to sit quietly – which was almost impossible – on the hard pew for a time which seemed like eternity and in a place where no-one would wish to spend eternity! I could not understand why my mother would look forward to those Sundays when Elwyn would be preaching, but look forward to them she did.

My mother died horrifically suddenly on her way home from Sunday School in May 1957, and I have a vague memory of Elwyn taking part in the funeral service at the cemetery of Bron-goch Anglican Church. In October 1958 we moved as a family to live in Bala High Street, and we were fellow members with Elwyn and his family until they moved to the south.

In 1962 I experienced God's grace at one of the Evangelical Movement's camps at Bryn-y-groes, their second headquarters in Bala since 1960. Through the camps and conferences of the Movement, and of the IVF afterwards, I would see Elwyn every now and again and he would always be interested in my career.

I remember a conversation during the summer of 1967 when I spent the holidays as a sub-warden of the Bryn-y-groes camps. That 1967 summer is significant in my story for during it I received my University degree and my wife. Maggie and I began courting during exam time and I asked her to marry me before the end of the term. During the summer holidays we agreed to marry in September before returning to college – Maggie to finish her Psychology degree and myself to begin a BD course. Our parents, quite naturally, were worrying that we were being rather impatient, to say the least! After all, we were only twenty years of age and had been courting for only a couple of months.

I don't remember exactly where or when I talked with Elwyn of my intention of getting married, but he was completely happy and positive about it. He knew that my sister, Haf, had looked after me since my mother's death when I was ten. He knew also that my father was not that careful of me, and that Haf, by 1967, had the responsibility of caring for her own family. What he told me was that I needed my own home, and that God had provided someone with whom I could begin to establish one. The fact that I am about to celebrate my forty-third year of extremely happy married life is a testament to his discernment.

Some years later he told me an interesting story of a particular visit of his to preach at Tyn-y-bont Chapel. As he prepared for that visit, God had not showed him what he should preach on. Clearly his method of preparing a sermon was to meditate and pray until he had an assurance in his heart that God had given him a word to deliver to the congregation. The work of the Holy Spirit in the ministry of preaching was not something theoretical to him. He expected to receive directly from God. But as he prepared for that particular Sunday at Tyn-y-bont, God was silent. Even when the time came for him to leave Bala for Tyn-y-bont, he had no idea what he should preach on. But as he passed Bron-goch Church, less than half a mile from Tyn-y-bont Chapel, the complete sermon was given to him. As he delivered this message, a few minutes after receiving it, he was convinced in his spirit that it was a message for my mother. If I remember correctly, what he told me was that my mother was the only person present that afternoon. He had received a direct message from God for my mother – and if he recollected correctly, this was about a fortnight before she died.

My mother had been raised in a believing home, for her father had received a deep experience of the Holy Spirit in the 1904 Revival. From what I have learned of her since I was myself converted, she was a believer from her youth. But I was greatly comforted from learning that she had received a special word from God to herself shortly before being called to his eternal presence. I don't remember whether or not I asked Elwyn as to the content of the message, but I suspect that he himself did not remember it. We must be satisfied with the knowledge that God also has his private messages to his people.

Dewi Arwel Hughes

Elwyn

J. Elwyn Davies and others had completed their pioneering work with the Evangelical Movement of Wales before I came to know him. I therefore joined an 'old' movement, one which had, at Bangor and the Gwendraeth Valley, already experienced the intensities of the initiatory thrill. A warmth of unity already existed amongst the group of young visionaries as to the centrality of the Bible and the classical foundations of the faith. This involved a profound seriousness with respect to man's pollution, to the need for the human spirit to be made alive so as to relate to God, and to the need for the heart to burn with gratitude at the knowledge that the Lord Jesus Christ had by his atonement paid with his blood for repentant sinners.

That is, there existed already a true God-defined ecumenicity amongst many young people in north and south Wales with respect to this new-old faith. This was the horizontal dimension, across two regions of Wales, of commitment to the Biblical gospel. A vertical ecumenicity existed also with the rich centuries of St David, Siôn Cent, Morgan Llwyd, Griffith Jones, Williams Pantycelyn, Daniel Rowland, Howell Harris, Thomas Charles, Thomas Jones, John Elias, Henry Rees, Owen Thomas and Martyn Lloyd-Jones. God therefore had quickened a vertical and horizontal Union in this country. And Elwyn Davies and others had established the *Cylchgrawn Efengylaidd* as a new voice to praise that True Faith. Retreats were held to teach the essentials of the gospel, and these developed into campaigns and conferences. A Fellowship and Movement existed therefore for other scattered fellowship-less Christians, here and there, who had dared to hold true to the eternal Biblical faith in spite of the growth of relativism, plurality and indifference. The Holy Spirit was at work in the heat of the general disintegration.

As a result, as an isolated evangelical Christian, I knew where I could turn to find consistency, trustworthiness, an experience of enthralling spiritual life, keen minds and a desire to fulfil the will of God. This, to me, was the importance of the work of Elwyn and others. In the very midst of religious vacillation with its institutionalised secularism, they had planted a garden for green shoots. They provided a fortress within which uncompromising believers could meet.

Providence had therefore ordained a young, gifted leader, J. Elwyn Davies, together with a group of truly spiritual helpers, and with a wise interpreter, Martyn Lloyd-Jones – like Griffith Jones, of old – at hand to inspire and advise. I became greatly indebted to Elwyn and to the new Movement for many blessings, and together they were the means used by God to bear much fruit in Wales. They were a blessing to us, both personally and as a family through the camps. I had many personal discussions with Elwyn and listened to many of his sermons; and I never left his company without a sense of Christ's presence with us.

But I wish to refer simply to one practical example. From time to time I would discuss with him the work of the Christian Union (amongst Aberystwyth students) and the weekly *Seiat* held in the same town. Because of the estrangement of belief amongst the Religious Establishment in Wales, in the wake of prejudices that do not need to be repeated here, what became progressively clearer was the severe famine and the intense longing amongst an increasing remnant of Christians, here and there, to feed from the pure streams of the truths of the Biblical faith, not according to secular human presumptions but according to the Word itself and to the understanding of strong believers through the ages. A robust fellowship was seriously needed. And in the Aberystwyth *Seiat* in the 60s it was believed, rightly or wrongly, that a small but real call existed amongst this Welsh-speaking group to step forward. I told Elwyn of the committed desire of the *Seiat* to establish other small societies similar to that in Aberystwyth, across Mid-Wales. I received an immediate, enthusiastic and practical response. We agreed that we as a *Seiat* and the Movement itself would be jointly responsible for a co-ordinator to set up the societies in Mid-Wales. Within a fortnight I received another call from Elwyn. He mentioned a young evangelist who was uncomfortable with the practices of his denomination, for various reasons, namely Gordon Macdonald. Gordon responded positively to the call. And after coming to Aberystwyth he, together with Rina his wife and three other families – John Ifor and Kitty Jones, Ieuan and Katie Jones, Wil and Jenny Morgan – established the Welsh Evangelical Church on 1 October 1967. By now (if we include the babies and those over eighty years of age) we are a substantial congregation with the majority under fifty years old.

Elwyn and his family have been full of practical interest in our work from that time. Subsequently a small stream of similar causes arose in Bangor, Colwyn Bay, Lampeter, Llangefni, Talsarnau, Tregaron and Waunfawr, and in Carmarthen. A similar spirit emerged within the English-speaking work, which had, by then, expanded within the Movement, and this proved fruitful in establishing many causes. Today, the work proceeds in co-operation, looking confidently towards the future, both because of the notable strengths of the Evangelical Theological College at Bryntirion, and of an increasing sense of the presence of God in thought, experience and will. But the Movement, in its beginnings, was through the medium of Welsh: its roots were deep in 'the Calvinistic civilisation' of the Welsh (as R. Tudur Jones would say). Great is our gratitude to Elwyn for guiding the organisation from its beginnings with care and loving benevolence.

I have considered here one critical example from amongst many, where Elwyn was seen, quietly but firmly, promoting the work of the Spirit to the glory of God. The precious friendship with Elwyn, and particularly the conversations between us, is and will always remain with me as one of the sweetest privileges of my life.

Bobi Jones

The earnest preacher and pastor

From *The Evangelical Magazine*, November/December 2007

Like many others throughout Wales, I regard Elwyn Davies as my father in the faith. Brought to Christ by means of his ministry, I had the inestimable privilege of having him as a pastor for several years when I was a young Christian, and later, it was he who received us as a family into membership at Free School Court Evangelical Church, Bridgend.

Many people have spoken and written about his vision and commitment to the gospel, his encouragement to individuals and to churches, his sound advice and wise guidance, and his spiritual insight into the needs of people in many different situations. All this we were privileged to witness and experience in Seion, Cwmafan, during the sixties.

The church was without a pastor when, in the providence of God, the Davies family came to live in the village in 1962. It was not long before he was invited to take over the preaching ministry, which he did in addition to his work as the General Secretary of the Evangelical Movement of Wales.

We who sat under his ministry from week to week remember his detailed expositions, delivered with warmth and earnestness which was often expressed with an urgent *'Clywch!'* ('Hear this!'). As he preached, the call of the gospel was made clear, and the conclusion that we should consider our position in the light of it was inescapable. This was powerful, Christ-exalting preaching. There are still those who, more than forty years later, remember particular sermons, and especially the series he preached on the Gospel of John. In Bible Studies he taught us to respect the Authority of the Scriptures and never to handle them lightly. In his gentle way, he would correct any slackness in our thinking by leading us to the logical conclusion of any remark made without due care, so that we could see the error for ourselves. Although his EMW work did not allow time for what he called a full-time pastoral ministry, it seemed to us that he did it anyway! The amount of personal work that he did was astounding, and many had cause to be thankful to God for the help and encouragement he gave. In this, as in all things, his beloved Mair was a constant, unfailing support.

Not all responded to the call of the gospel, but no-one was in any doubt about the godliness that was evident in them both. We were truly blessed by their presence among us.

Menna Thomas

Sharing a longing

I first met Mr and Mrs Davies in 1978 when I was invited to the ministers' fraternal at Bridgend. I was the young minister of Bethlehem Pentecostal Church, Cefncribwr, and though not a Pentecostal myself I mixed among the men as something of an 'outsider'. From the start Elwyn welcomed, encouraged, defended and affirmed me in every way. He became something of a spiritual father. We went to the Bala Ministers' Conference together, and slowly his influence rubbed off on me.

I came to share his longing to see all evangelicals, Reformed and Charismatic, grow in respect, unity and truth. He was troubled by the tendency of ministers and churches to separate themselves in small groups apart from those with whom they should be in Gospel fellowship. His work of ensuring that the Apostolic Church became part of the British Evangelical Council (now Affinity) was typical of him. I still do not know how he did it.

'We have also to remember our brethren who are in Pentecostal and charismatic church groupings. Are we not to apply the principles that are to govern our relationships to one another as Christians to them also?'

We shared a deep desire to see and feel the Holy Spirit's presence and power in our lives and churches. The impact of the events in Dolgellau in January 1948, when the Holy Spirit came so powerfully on the group of young people, left a permanent mark. A vision and prophecy that told of the coming movement and influence across Wales left him longing for His presence and power.

'We are to pray for Revival but we are to pray also for the Lord's presence and power to the degree that He will see fit to grant it to His people every day, and go on praying for this constantly.'

A Father in the Faith

Dr Lloyd-Jones gave his encouragements after his own experiences at Bristol and Bala in 1949.

Elwyn Davies also instilled in me a sense of Wales's glorious past, in a Gospel sense, and a concern to see churches prosper across the nation. He had seen small groups established, evangelistic missions conducted, and an increase in the influence of Biblical authority and of the Gospel, and he longed to see it again. He spoke with regret and pain of the division and isolation that policies of 'non-association' with fellow-evangelicals in the denominations had caused.

After I came back to Wales in 1998, was learning Welsh and working with churches and leaders across Wales, I often called at Ar-y-bryn, Carmarthen. We talked of the needs, issues and signs of hope in Wales, and discussed his current writings, especially those on themes of evangelical unity from John's Gospel. I think he felt that his son had come of age.

David Ollerton
David Ollerton is a minister, preacher, and leader in church planting.
He is one of the founders of the Wales Wide Christian network.

The quintessence of graciousness

From *The Evangelical Magazine*, November/December 2007

I rang a friend in England to tell him of Elwyn's death and, after a note of sympathy, he said, 'Elwyn, the quintessence of graciousness'. I think this is how many of us will remember him. He was very much a people person, and when talking to you it was as if he had all the time in the world to give to you. He would listen thoughtfully and patiently, ask a few questions, and then in his quiet un-dogmatic way, suggest a solution. Sometimes you would hear what you didn't want to hear, because Elwyn could be both wise and honest. You could always be assured of a sympathetic hearing. He listened very much as a brother or a father, depending on your age! You knew that when he said he would remember you in prayer that he would do just that.

To hear him pray was always a blessing. Hearing him address God in that gentle, slightly hoarse voice, as 'Heavenly Father' made you realise that here was a man who really knew God. In his praying he could take you into the presence of God. Someone who worked alongside him said that it was not uncommon when you knocked on his door and opened it, to find him on his knees.

Elwyn moved in many circles and touched many lives. We thank God for every remembrance of him.

Derek Swann

A discerning heart

I remember a young student in his first year at Swansea University joining, rather shyly, a small group that was meeting in a bed-sit in the Uplands area of the city. This was towards the end of the spring of 1970, and the meeting had been arranged by some of the young people of Bethany Chapel, Ammanford, who were also students at the college. They had invited the Rev. Elwyn Davies to lead them, and he was willing enough to give up an evening in order to travel to Swansea and to address a handful of youngsters. The student was shy because he was not familiar with evangelical people. He had been raised in a fairly liberal chapel and did not have much of an idea what to expect from a Bible study in a bed-sit. But he had had to acknowledge that a particular certainty and truth, that was not part of his experience, was evident in the Christianity of his new friends.

Mr Davies began to talk on the Beatitudes, in a way that was quite new to the student. He spoke of them, not as some idealistic goals to be aimed at, and not as various descriptions of different godly individuals, but as experiences common to all Christians – being poor in spirit from an awareness of spiritual poverty, mourning for sin, increasing in meekness and mercy as those who know what it is to depend daily on forgiveness, hungering for inward righteousness to take the place of the natural hypocrisy and pollution. And as he listened, the student realised for the first time the meaning of the phrase: *'awdurdodol eiriau'r nef'* ('authoritative words of heaven').[72] On hearing the simple, yet profound, exposition of the familiar verses it was impossible not to believe that this, of course, was their meaning, and that they were wholly relevant and personal, and more important than anything else in the world. This indeed was the Christian life, though not yet anything that he had experienced.

Then, producing a thrill of terror in his heart, Mr Davies began to question the eight or nine who were present on their experiences. He conversed with them gently and leisurely, drawing from them the story of their conversions and the ebb and flow of their spiritual lives. He passed from one to another around the circle and the boy squirmed inwardly as he tried to decide what to do. Should he lie and seek to imitate the words of the others, or acknowledge what he had not known himself before, that the experiences of the Christian were quite unknown to him?

The questioning arrived at the next to him in the circle and she mentioned the comfort she received from the words of hymns. Mr Davies took up the theme and proceeded to describe that wonderful change that took place in the new convert, when the familiar but quite inexplicable words and phrases suddenly became crystal clear and an explanation and description of the most personal experiences. The student realised, with an intense relief, that the questioning was not to be resumed, and that a door of escape had opened up before him.

I do not remember anything else of that evening, but I have often wondered since whether Mr Davies had discerned the situation fully and had ensured that no-one would be embarrassed. That would have been completely typical of him.

John Aaron

Indebted to Elwyn Davies

From *Y Cylchgrawn Efengylaidd*, October 2007

My first memory of the Rev. Elwyn Davies is very clear in my mind. I had come to an experience of the Lord and of his mercy on my own and after a difficult period of soul-searching. I understood very little of the truths of the faith at the time – I only knew that God had forgiven me, and that he called me to serve him.

About ten days after this stirring experience I found myself at Bryn-y-groes, amongst a group of students from Bangor. The occasion was the November Retreat of 1973, with Mr Davies preaching. He took us to John's Gospel, and his every word was food to a hungry soul. As was his practice, his sermon was long, explaining the Bible very carefully – not what you would expect to appeal to young people. But this was a period of blessing amongst the students of Aberystwyth and Bangor colleges. To me it was an opening of a door into a new world, where the Bible was the key to the great secrets of God, and into the secret of living as his children in this world. I heard him many times during this period, at retreats and at conferences in Bala-Bangor College.

Doctrine and experience

We were shown that the Bible was not a disconnected collection of the writings of men in their seeking after God. On the contrary, this was the trustworthy revelation of God concerning himself and his salvation in his Son, Jesus Christ. The great doctrines of grace were presented to us, and we realised that we belonged to a wonderful tradition. We could trace our spiritual roots through our Welsh nonconformist Fathers. We were brought to an understanding that Calvinism at its best was not an old, irrelevant, worn-out system, but the living and powerful Christianity of the New Testament. As we considered the doctrine of sin, we saw the deceit and cunning of our own hearts. As we heard of election, the incomparable grace of God came to the fore, and we were fired with the desire to reach others with this message. That there is an experiential element in all this was emphasised, and prayer became something more than the recital of words. It was an essential direct line to our Father in heaven. No-one who heard Elwyn Davies, lifting his face heavenwards, saying 'Our Father', was in any doubt that he was speaking with the holy, gracious, living One. In this way, a generation of us became aware that prayer, meditation in the Word and sitting under the Word through the hearing of true preaching, were central to a healthy spiritual life.

Another great burden upon his heart was the unity of evangelical Christians. He would rejoice to see a group of us of differing backgrounds joining together to evangelise at the Eisteddfod, or at the Conference in Aberystwyth. His personal support and advice was of great help to me, a minister with the Presbyterians, in one of the traditional denominations, at the time when I moved to serve in the Evangelical Church at Bangor. When the AECW (Associating Evangelical Churches of Wales) was formed, bringing evangelical churches into an association, he worked unsparingly to ensure that there would be no turning away from those who were not able to unite with that association.

Then there was the committee work. In the words of the late Rev. Gareth Davies, 'Committee work is not a waste of time, but a discipline to be exercised for the benefit of the kingdom.' As I was drawn in to the committees of the Evangelical Movement, I came to appreciate Elwyn Davies's burden for Wales. He believed passionately that Wales's need was to regain her hold on that gospel which had been her glory and security throughout the centuries. And if this necessitated spending many days in discussion and planning in committee, then so be it.

Longing for revival

In all this there was the realisation that none of our efforts would succeed without the Lord's blessing. Therefore, alongside all the activity was the longing for revival. And for him, revival was not a *'man gwyn fan draw'* [some perfect place over yonder]. It was, rather, the drawing near of God to his people in mercy, and that mercy overflowing to others as Christ was revealed to them more clearly.

He did not see the answering of his prayers for revival, but he believed, with those others who had laboured together with him, that his prayers and efforts were not in vain. As he relinquished the work into the hands of others he believed that its fruit would yet be seen, and that the Spirit would yet be experienced traversing the land. And this is the challenge for us as we face our generation. Do we long to see Christ as Lord in the hearts of our fellow-Welshmen? If so, are we ready to bear the torch that he carried and to hold it high, so that our Wales will hear of the great works of God?

We are grateful for having known him, and may the Kingdom for which he laboured diligently flourish again in our day.

Dafydd Job

Evangelist

One sad result for me of being a student in the 1970s was that liberal theology had produced times of 'dry, comfortless, dark, confusing unbelief...'. The visits of Elwyn Davies to the Christian Union, to Ebenezer Church, Bangor, and to Bryn-y-groes retreats were a means of grace for many of us. The reality of his personal devotion, the freshness of his detailed and discerning exposition of God's Word were the means of reviving our affections towards God our Father and the Lord Jesus Christ.

But for me, without doubt, being present at the *seiadau* of the period at Bryn-y-groes under Mr Davies's leadership provided an ever-memorable experience. I remember one in particular where many had suggested topics to discuss. But when one young girl shared honestly her spiritual battles over assurance, Mr Davies took up the theme. For about an hour and a half we had a true experience meeting under the careful, firm and pastoral leadership of Elwyn Davies.

To see a spiritual pastor at his work was a means of grace. He corrected us, quoting, with fondness, various verses or portions of Scripture as a basis for what he said. He respected every contribution. Warnings, encouragements and the sharing of personal experiences – these all wonderfully merged together in the careful hands of the *seiat's* leader. One thing that struck me at that meeting, and that was confirmed to me every time I met him, whether in a public preaching service, at the office in Bryntirion, at a ministers' conference or in personal conversation, was his wholly humble and unassuming nature, though committed in his principles and counsels. Humility is the most beautiful attire of God's servants. To see Elwyn Davies demonstrating this virtue in such a consistently unostentatious way was a challenge to those of us who were young men with an eye to the ministry, where pride and self-esteem so easily lurk.

His advice was always wholly Biblical but without disregarding elements that others might ignore. I remember the time I sought his advice on a matter and he began the conversation by stating how important it was not to forget Freud and his emphasis on the early experiences of childhood, particularly in one's relationship, or lack of relationship, with one's parents. He proceeded to enumerate many possibilities as we understand ourselves and others around us. But the prayer at the close of our conversation emphasised clearly that it is in fellowship with God through his Son that we truly understand our situation and identity in this world and that which is to come.

It would be easy to conclude that Elwyn Davies was an able expositor and theologian, while possessing few other gifts. However, I remember a night during the Loughor Eisteddfod when he revealed the heart of a passionate evangelist. I was leading an early evening open-air meeting in Gowerton Square, and Mr Davies offered himself to preach briefly! He had just noticed a box of matches thrown on to the pavement with a motto on it noting how short is our life in this world. I presumed to remind him that the message was not to be more than five minutes.

He smiled and proceeded with a passionate warning and exhortation for those who were passing by that to seek God was their privilege and responsibility – indeed, God was at work seeking them. As he finished and handed the microphone over to me, he smiled again and said, looking at his watch, 'Four minutes thirty seconds, Mr Thomas!' We went on to an evangelistic service in a nearby chapel where Mr Davies preached on the verse, 'Worthy is the Lamb'. The main characteristics of the good news preached that night were passion, simplicity, present-day relevance and Christ-centrality, as the evangelist pressed us to deny every human merit and to trust alone in the perfect worthiness given by God himself. I felt that night that the gospel was the heart and meaning of life to this man. I have no shame in confessing that he is one of my greatest heroes.

Meirion Thomas

Elwyn Davies and the BEC

'Bala? Isn't that the place near Snowdon to which young Mary Jones walked for her Welsh Bible?'

If the name means anything at all to them, that is probably as much as many Christians outside Wales know about Bala. No more than a name on a map. For a good number of evangelical pastors in England, however, the name Bala conjures up something quite distinctive. Over many years now the English Ministers' Conference of the Evangelical Movement of Wales, held at Bryn-y-groes in June, has been a blessing to visiting pastors from outside Wales. For some of them, Bala became as essential a fixture in their diary as the Banner or Carey Conferences. In the 1960s and 70s, of course, for men living too far from London to attend the Westminster Fellowship, it was an opportunity to benefit from the unique ministry and interactive teaching style of Dr Martyn Lloyd-Jones. That factor alone was a sufficient draw for some of them. But even after the Doctor's home-call in 1981 there were devotees who kept coming to the Bala Conference. It was not the luxury of single en-suite bedrooms or guaranteed sunshine for the afternoon outings that drew them! It was rather that they experienced there something they did not find in any other such gathering.

Up to 1982 my three pastorates had all been in England, so one of the first tasks I faced in becoming General Secretary of the British Evangelical Council (BEC) was to get to know its various constituent bodies in England, Scotland, Northern Ireland and, of course, Wales. For some years I had served on the council of the Fellowship of Independent Evangelical Churches (FIEC) and had got to know a few EMW men, some of whom came regularly to the Westminster Fellowship, which I had attended for 24 years. No-one benefitting from the Doctor's ministry during those intense debates over ecumenism and evangelical church unity in the 60s and 70s could have failed to learn a good deal about the situation in Wales, and the role being played by the EMW. Up to 1982, however, although I had met Elwyn on several occasions, I had had no direct fellowship with him.

But during the period I served the BEC, I can testify that his friendship became a significant blessing.

From the outset, he was insistent: *'If you want to get to know the Movement, then you must come to Bala!'* So it was that in June 1983 I joined the Bala regulars and began to taste that which kept them coming. Elwyn also arranged that I should share his room, which meant that I shared his personal prayers and experienced at close quarters the priorities which had made him such an influential Christian leader. By this time the Doctor was no longer with us and, to be honest, I cannot today recall the names of any of the speakers, nor the topics we discussed. What I can recall is the concern of Elwyn and the men at Bala to give me a taste of their unique heritage, something far less well-known in England.

I have been asked to trace the influence Elwyn had on the evangelical scene outside Wales. We had overlapped in our service as General Secretaries of EMW and BEC, respectively, for only eight years (1982-1990) when he retired from his role. I am sure, however, that the following points were characteristic of his influence over a much longer period.

In my view, Elwyn maintained a healthy balance between concern for the revival of the church and concern for the reformation of the church. Alongside his personal faith, his clear Christian mind, his genuine warmth and his historical perspectives, it was this balance which made the strongest impression on me and, I believe, on those in England who knew him. It was this which was the ethos of the Bala conference and which brought men from England to it year by year. Both topics were being pursued without either being neglected.

The reforming aspect was hugely important to church relations during those years. Post-war ecumenism was fed by an increasingly confident liberal theology in the major denominations. A fear of declining numbers and reduced influence was driving church leaders to reconsider their priorities, and evangelicals were having to face questions about their own position. We all discovered that we had not given sufficient thought to what constituted a consistent evangelical ecclesiology. We had a lot of work to do. There is no need to rehearse here the events of 1966 and the subsequent tensions between free church and Anglican evangelicals, other than to say that similar challenges faced other major denominations also. The role of Dr Martyn Lloyd-Jones in this is well known, although not as widely understood as it should be. It was natural that Elwyn's friendship with the Doctor, and the close affinity of their thinking, meant that both were active in working towards practical solutions to these dilemmas. It was in 1967, when Westminster Chapel joined the FIEC and formally identified itself with the BEC, that EMW also responded positively to an approach to join the BEC. The aim was to further the reforming of the church, or at least the relationships between local churches and the bodies in which they were grouped. Elwyn became a prominent representative of the EMW on the BEC Executive, and was appointed chairman from 1969 to 1971. He promoted attempts, regrettably with little success at the time, to apply BEC principles at grass roots by the formation of local councils of evangelical churches and local ministers' fraternals. During the whole of my period with the BEC this was clearly a work close to his heart. We held two major conferences in Wales, in Wrexham in 1984 and in Cardiff in 1991.

In fact, the EMW has never been merely a church body but a movement serving evangelical ministers, whether within doctrinally-mixed denominations or in separated churches. Its ministers' fraternals, embracing men in both situations, has always been one of its strengths. During the period under review, the BEC became more overtly a council of churches, in order to distinguish itself further from the Evangelical Alliance, where participation in ecumenism was no barrier to personal membership. In our BEC discussions, however, Elwyn always balanced his commitment to a gospel-based church unity with a warm pastoral concern for men and churches who had not yet broken their denominational ties.

The yearning for revival was also never far from Elwyn's heart or conversation, however. And this priority was shared by an Englishman who was to become a key figure in Elwyn's influence outside Wales, namely, the Rev. Hon. Roland Lamb. Their friendship began while Roland was serving the IVF, as it was then, and was deepened when he became a Methodist minister in Aberystwyth, exercising an influential gospel ministry among students there. After he left Methodism on grounds of conscience, he became part-time Secretary of the BEC. Elwyn was one of those who later urged him in 1967 to devote his whole time to that work and who offered consistent support and encouragement to him through the years. They became life-long friends, and in their subsequent ministries Elwyn and Roland showed that their common concern was not for nationwide evangelical church unity as an end in itself, but as a step of obedience which might prepare God's people for a fresh outpouring of the Spirit in our generation.

Why some reformed Anglicans in England have been less than enthusiastic about the concern for revival prominent in the Doctor and Elwyn is not easy to explain. Behind the jibes about 'Celtic emotionalism' there seems to be a genuine fear that stressing the subjective work of the Holy Spirit in the preacher himself could endanger the objective reality of the Spirit's work in the Scripture from which he preaches. Some also seem troubled that while we are waiting (and praying) for a time of revival it is too easy for us to neglect the pressing challenge of a lost generation and a corrupt society. It is to Elwyn's great credit, however, that I never found him guilty of such aberrations.

I myself can testify to two specific examples which run counter to these implied charges. For several years before my BEC appointment, I chaired the FIEC Citizenship Committee, a group researching into and recommending resources for evangelical pastors on social issues. It had, for example, proved exceptionally valuable when the Aids crisis emerged, finding many of us ill prepared to answer the homosexuality issues being raised. During that period we benefitted greatly from arrangements made by Elwyn for representatives from the EMW to be co-opted on to our committee in England.

The other example relates to gospel work among children. I had been part of an FIEC group which reviewed the provision of Sunday School lesson schemes available in the UK. We were disappointed at what we found and the outcome was the founding of Go Teach Publications, which has been providing Bible-based materials for Sunday Schools and Holiday Clubs over many generations. Go Teach has benefitted hugely from EMW members on its board and from EMW contributors to its ministry.

Neither of these significantly influential initiatives outside Wales would have been possible without Elwyn's backing. His heritage of experiential spirituality was always matched by a profound concern for a relevant testimony and a deep longing to reach the lost.

Alan Gibson
General Secretary of the British Evangelical Council from 1982 to 1999.

A family man

From *The Evangelical Magazine*, June/July 1990

I must confess that it is not easy to respond to the Editor's request to write a word about my father – mainly because I know that the idea would be completely against his wishes. Although my father was a public figure, yet he is a very private person, one who would be very unhappy at drawing attention to himself in any way. Yet, I will attempt to do so, if only to acknowledge publicly our privilege as children in having such an exceptional father.

To those unacquainted with my father, I would like to present him as one who was always more than ready to exhibit his talents with a football on the lawn at home in Cwmafan. He followed his course as the General Secretary of the Movement – to the great loss of the Welsh national football team!

He would often tease us when we were young. I remember talking to him once in the car while we waited for my mother to come from the surgery. We were discussing clothes, and I was echoing the teenage point of view at the time – that it did not matter how one was dressed. Suddenly he drew my attention to a young man passing by dressed as a punk rocker. 'That's the new local minister,' he said. 'No!' I replied (looking at his clothes). 'Why not?' asked my father. 'I thought that clothes did not matter.' And that was the end of my argument.

Our father was very loyal to us as children, greatly concerned for the six of us – each one as much as the others. He discussed the issues of the day with us, revealing his wide knowledge and wise views on matters of importance. He taught each of us to think for ourselves and to see the excellence of the Christian faith over all other ways of life.

His life was a very busy one because of his responsibilities with the Evangelical Movement and for the churches under his care. In his absence it fell to my mother to control and discipline the six of us – quite a task! – and to enlighten him when he returned home of our behaviour during the day.

My father would maintain family worship in the home, teaching us constantly of the truths and values of the Christian faith. He did so without laying any pressure upon us to believe but rather encouraging us to seek God's face for ourselves.

The greatest influence upon us as children was the practical, humble and conscientious way in which our parents applied the faith to their own lives. We remember with warmth and gratitude their high standards, their burden in prayer for a spiritual revival in our country, their practical care for the work of God's children throughout Wales (without forgetting missionaries), their hospitality, and their gentleness towards those in need. All this made a great impression upon us – an impression that was an undeniable witness for us to follow in their footsteps.

An experience at a schoolfriend's party when I was 17 crystallised that impression for me. (I had made a profession of faith when I was 13, but this reinforced my belief that I had chosen the right path.) A group of us from Rhydfelen Sixth Form attended a party one Saturday night. Having arrived and greeted the others, I was shocked and disappointed when I saw the lax and irresponsible behaviour of some of my closest friends at school. What struck me most was the realisation of how the people of the world enjoyed themselves, and of how superficial and empty that enjoyment was. What 'the world' offered was so insubstantial and sad. I could not avoid the conclusion. Standing in the midst of the merry-making of the party, all I could think of were the values my parents had taught me.

I remembered the close, respectful and warm relationship of my parents, and their concern for us as children. I decided there and then to refuse the embrace of the world and its temptations, and to own and embrace the faith and values of my parents, in that I had seen the benefit and practicality of their faith in the experiences and trials of life.

I only stayed at the party for half an hour but that was enough for me to appreciate what I had received from my parents. I hitch-hiked back from Caerphilly to Cwmafan – thankful for a Christian home to return to.

Tributes and Reminiscences

My father would relate to each one of us children as individuals, neither favouring any one above the others nor dealing with us as if we were all the same. The six of us can remember many, many occasions when his counsel was above price. I remember him comforting me one summer in Aberystwyth when I had heard that I had failed some exams in school. He consoled me with the words, 'We must believe in the way ordained for you.' And twenty years later I can thank God for his wise and timely advice.

I thank God that he blessed us with such a wise, loving and gentle father, and a mother that meant so much to him and to ourselves, and with parents who, together, were so committed to the cause of Jesus Christ in our country.

In that no-one's upbringing is perfect, it would be irresponsible of me to romanticise about the past. Yet our earthly father succeeded in teaching us 'in the way of wisdom' and we were led 'in right paths' (Proverbs 4:11). And we thank our heavenly Father for the privilege of such an upbringing.

Hywel Meredydd Davies

The Spirit and the Truth

I remember the first time I saw him. I became a Christian in February 1984. I had come to the Conference for a day. Elwyn and Mair were sitting on the Prom and Joan Derrick from Pontardulais introduced me to him. I remember him saying, 'I knew of you a long time before you were converted.' This was through the Rev. Arthur Pritchard. Mr Pritchard had known, it seems, that I had been under conviction for some time. And thus, Elwyn Davies knew.

Later, in August 1986 and earlier, Mr Davies came to Noddfa, Pontardulais. There were about eight or ten of us in the congregation. What struck us was this – that he insisted that you understood what he had to say. He would see a puzzled look on my face. 'Did you understand that, Eira?' And in my notes I can find many things which I had written down more than once. I learnt so much from him at that time.

I remember one service in particular. His text was 'He shall convict the world of sin.' And I was deeply convicted. Although I tried to take some notes, it came to a point where I could write no more through feeling so unworthy, as he proclaimed the love of Christ. There was nothing of himself in the preaching, only the love of Christ.

During his visits to us, he went through Matthew's Gospel, and then through John's Gospel. He clearly loved John's Gospel, as you know. He emphasised in particular the conviction of sin, of righteousness and of judgement. And in one service the Holy Spirit came down. I was quite overcome.

He served at Noddfa for a period of three months initially. This became six months, and then nine months. It was a very special time. And of course, we remained friends after that period.

You cannot bring yourself to a conviction of sin. This is something to which man is blind. It is only the Spirit who can show us – by convicting us. And he shows us also how lost those around us are, and that only conviction of sin can bring them to Christ. This is what overcame me, and it remains with me today, for without a conviction of sin people do not truly appreciate what the Lord has done for them.

A blessing certainly rested over Noddfa during that period. Some came to life. And Noddfa grew from that time onwards. I am very grateful to Elwyn Davies and Arthur Pritchard. In a short time I was taught the great truths. And instead of living on my experiences, I was shown my experience in the Scriptures.

Eira Jones

A few impressions

John Emyr is married to Gwen, Elwyn Davies' eldest daughter.

When the news broke of the departure of John Elwyn Davies, numerous sympathising messages were sent to members of his family, and many of them conveyed how much the life of this friend and minister had meant to the letter-writer. One friend from Italy, for example, wrote, 'I remember how he, with a true fatherly care, was anxious for me and took care of my soul...'. Many who had the privilege of knowing him had the same testimony: he was interested in you – you, yourself, in your true unconcealed state – inexhaustibly interested, and you knew that his interest was sincere, without hypocrisy and full of good will.

One of my earliest memories of him is the one I noted (in the *Cylchgrawn Efengylaidd*) in 1974. He was the guest speaker during a retreat at Bryn-y-groes, and I understood as I listened to him (as a proud and critical student) that as an ambassador he was a true member of that '*torf ardderchog*'[73] of evangelists that had traversed Wales through the centuries, but were now increasingly rare. The content of his message, the parable of the sower, was of course important. His method of preaching was also striking. His interest in the gospel was not peripheral, uninvolved or indifferent. It was the essence and purpose of his being, and this was to be heard in his voice and seen in his face and his whole bearing as he preached. To him, to preach the good news and to present Jesus Christ to others was not a common activity amongst other relatively unimportant activities. This task, preaching and fulfilling the other duties of a minister of souls, was what gave him deep satisfaction and a sense of vocation – more satisfaction than the administrative duties that accompanied his role as leader of the Evangelical Movement of Wales, though they also had their place.

He was gifted with a remarkable ability for making friends. Towards the end of the Second World War, for example, he befriended a German soldier called Ekkehard, who had been a prisoner of war. Ekkehard is mentioned in the introduction to the volume *O! Ryfedd Ras [O! Wondrous*

Grace] (1998), in which Elwyn Davies speaks of his conversion which occurred at that time. A deep friendship developed between them, and many years later that friendship still flourished. When my wife, Gwen, and I visited Ekkehard's home in East Berlin for a few days in October 1996, the welcome we received from the ex-prisoner (who had contributed over the years to the economic recovery of his country) was effusive because of his appreciation of that friendship with my father-in-law.

Elwyn Davies was the first to acknowledge at all times how indebted he was to his partner, Mair Eluned Davies. Since the romantic days of their first friendship in the University College of North Wales, Bangor, and then in the enchanting atmosphere of the farmhouse of their life-long friends John and Mari Jones in Llanymawddwy, Mair was his muse and his greatest supporter. Together their partnership was as strong as that three-fold cord that cannot be broken, and to visit their home over the years was, for myself at any rate, like visiting a university of experience. You departed from there with your mental capacities full, and with strength and sustenance to face life.

The family meant much to him, and this was seen in his practical kindness to each of his children, children-in-law, and grandchildren. A wife and family have the means of judging the true nature of a man, when at home as well as when in the public eye, and in response to my questions I obtained the following comments from Mair Eluned Davies:

Humility
He had the energy and determination to carry forward a pioneering work, but he would always consider himself as a member of a team of brethren, and his great emphasis always was for mutual love and unity. (He summarised many of his insights on Christian unity in his booklet *Striving Together: The Evangelical Movement of Wales – its principles and aims* (1984).)

Spiritual perception
As he pursued his day-to-day work, he was always alive to the possibility of discovering those who possessed leadership material, and he would spend time with them. He asked them to serve on regional committees, ministerial circles, etc. He believed that God called people to the work

of his Kingdom but that they had to be discovered, that time had to be spent with them, and that they should be regularly supported.

A careful listener
He was always ready to provide an ear to those beset with problems. He would never refuse or excuse himself. He had the heart of a pastor and the gift of getting to the root of problems and issues.

An unshakeable commitment to the Welsh language
In days when there was not so much talk of bilingualism, he was convinced that all the activities of the Movement should be bilingual. Some ministers in the early years thought that the Conference in Aberystwyth should be in English (in that all understood that language). But many Welsh speakers insisted that there had to be a Welsh Conference. Without much equipment and resources, considerable work and commitment were needed to ensure that the Welsh provision had its fair share.

Concentrating on the essential
You could not be long in his company without realising that he was a person who concentrated on the essentials of spiritual life. How may the individual Christian live a life of fellowship with God? How may we know clear guidance? It was because of such considerations as these that the Gospel of John became so crucially important. (The pages of his Bible are worn thin in parts of this Gospel, chapters 14-17 particularly.) He would note that Jesus Christ had spent hours in prayer to his heavenly Father, and that in his public ministry he would do the works that the Father had commanded him to do 'in his name'. We also, as the disciples of the Master, should spend time in prayer (as individuals and as churches) seeking to know the will of God. (He would admire those who would set apart a day of prayer before holding an important committee the next day.)

At heart, he was a man of one vision – strong in his principles and very alert to any emphases that might harm the evangelical faith. He would always respond positively to any reasonable request to speak, on radio or television. (I was always amazed at his readiness to do this, knowing how tired he was at times.) When he was about the work of the Movement he would often be called upon to defend the evangelical faith, and he would always do so courteously but firmly, with unequivocal conviction.

Praying for spiritual blessing

He respected the judgement and leadership of Dr Martyn Lloyd-Jones who regularly attended the Ministers' Conference at Bala. He would acknowledge also the influence of Pastor George Griffiths and the company at Cwm-twrch. For many years he attended a prayer meeting for revival, held on Friday mornings under the Pastor's leadership. Elwyn would often read the histories of the revivals of the past. This emphasis was never forgotten by him.

Evangelical unity

Elwyn worked diligently for this cause. There should be no separation, he would say, over secondary issues. He was always very fair to his brethren in the denominational churches, amongst whom were some of his closest friends. He wished all to be in agreement.

A fair and balanced judgement

He would be always thinking and meditating, and was a clear and logical thinker. He loved music, football and walking, and, to a degree, was interested in politics. But he could never truly relax with any interest or hobby. He was 'a man of one Book', as Daniel Owen used to say of the old saint Dafydd Dafis.

Appreciating fellow-labourers

He would appreciate the efforts of all who put their shoulders to the work, and was particularly grateful for the commitment of those like Brenda Lewis and Mair Jones who laboured with him in the office over the years.

*   *   *   *   *   *   *   *   *   *   *   *   *   *   *   *   *   *

For all our sadness as a family as he faced his last illness, the times spent by members of the family and by friends in his company was very precious. The residents' home, Brynderwen, (near Carmarthen) where he spent some weeks before crossing the river, is a building very like those that he and his co-workers secured for the work of the Kingdom in Wales: Eryl Aran and Bryn-y-groes in Bala and Bryntirion in Bridgend. He was happy therefore at Brynderwen, but at times would be low in spirit, and on these occasions there would be no trace of a smile upon his face. On one of my last visits, when he by then could hardly talk, I tried to think of something that would cheer him. I thought of the evangelistic campaign that he led at Trefor in Arfon at the end of the 1940s, before I was born. It was during that campaign that my father, Emyr Roberts (a minister in Trefor at the time) and my mother were saved. I spoke of this; he listened for a while and a smile, like sunshine breaking through the clouds, came to his lips.

Some days later, when we realised that the end was near, a ministerial friend, the Rev. Geraint Morse, came to pray with him. In great weakness, Elwyn Davies also prayed. This was his last prayer, and it was a prayer for Wales. On the last afternoon, with Geraint Morse praying, and committing him to the care of the angelic hosts, he crossed over.

Because of his musical gifts, the praise in his soul and his burden for revival, hymns - in English and in Welsh - were a source of great comfort to Elwyn Davies. He used to listen to them at the end of a day before sleeping. And it was to the accompaniment of the great hymns that he departed this life. One of them was that prayer of petition which had been a means of blessing at the beginning of his career, both for him and Mair and the happy company who had shared his enthusiasm and hope in the halcyon days at Llanymawddwy. The following are the first and last verses of that hymn:

Ddiddanydd anfonedig nef,
  fendigaid Ysbryd Glân,
hiraethwn am yr awel gref
  a'r tafod tân.

O heaven-sent Comforter,
blessed Holy Spirit;
we long for the strong breeze
and the tongues of fire.

Rho'r hyder anorchfygol gynt
  ddilynai'r tafod tân;
chwyth dros y byd fel nerthol wynt,
  O Ysbryd Glân.

Give that unconquerable confidence
that accompanied the tongues of fire;
blow over the world as a powerful wind,
O Holy Spirit.

John Emyr

Articles

by J. Elwyn Davies

Amongst Berlin's ruins
A picture of misery

Berlin, Tuesday
Some six months ago, as I said goodbye to a prisoner of war who was returning to Germany, I told him to prepare himself for disappointment and distress.

It was in the same spirit that I came here to Berlin, expecting and fearing the worst. Some days ago I walked through the ruins of Berlin in the ex-prisoner's company. He smiled quietly when I told him that I had never imagined that the circumstances were so bad, and that I had no idea how the inhabitants could have lived through them.

At home in Wales we tend to believe that circumstances are quickly improving in Germany, and if we have assisted in any way in campaigns of support for the Continent, after two years of 'peace' we begin to be complacent. We accept false reports that claim that all is well in Germany – 'anything may be bought on the black market' – and we stop sending our contributions to the *Faner's* Fund, or to sending our clothes to some poor home in Hamburg or Hannover. If there was a need of help for the people of Germany, there is greater need now than ever before.

The pitiful ration
Since the end of the war the population has had to live on some one and a half thousand calories a day per head, or more generally on some thousand calories a day; sometimes eight hundred calories or less. I can assure you that this is completely true.

Perhaps these figures do not convey much to you, not even if I were to add the fact that we in Britain consume on average some three thousand calories of food a day. But what if we were to translate the figure 'a thousand and a half calories' into the equivalent foodstuff, and what if you, a mother or wife in Wales, were asked to prepare three meals a day from the following resources:

Every German is allowed 400 grams of bread a day, that is, a little less than a pound a day, and the same amount of potato; 10 grams of butter or margarine (almost invariably the latter), that is, an ounce every three days, or a little over two and a quarter ounces a week; some 40 grams of meat, a little less than a pound every ten days, and the same amount of flour; some 20 grams of sugar, that is, a pound in a little over three weeks.

And that is all, literally.

Tins or fish or food may not be bought unrationed as done in Britain; things that we take for granted, jam, bacon, meat paste or similar, are unheard of here. Every meal, every day, must be prepared from the above list. The only variation is that the 40 grams of meat per day may be exchanged for 40 grams of peas.

And to add to the suffering, it is generally the case that the people do not receive their full ration, either because the shopkeeper, butcher or baker, defraud them – I know for a fact that this is true – or because the promise is not kept due to the scarcity of food.

The meals
Can you imagine what this means, for children, for students, for workmen, for the old? On one day, for breakfast they have a slice or two of dry bread, for dinner only a few potatoes or dry bread, and for supper the ubiquitous 'soup'. On another day, a slice of bread for breakfast – if there is any left after about five days of the week, the 'soup' for dinner and a few potatoes at evening. And so on every day, throughout the last two years, for today, and for the winter ahead of them.

The workman receives a little more bread and meat, but the difference is not worth mentioning – with the result that young and old women are seen working their fingers to the bone clearing and cleaning bricks in the midst of the dust of the ruins, hoping to win the 'workman's food token'. It is pitiful to see them; they expend as much energy in their work as they will earn in calories for their labour. But what else can a mother do if her child is perishing before her eyes?

Most of the population have succeeded in adding to their own weekly ration by buying food on the black market. If that were not the case, they would not be alive today. According to official figures, 87% are faithful customers of the black market, but all resort to it, sooner or later. There is no other option except dying. That is the truth: while such scarcity of food and goods persist, the black market is inevitable and dealing in it a necessity.

Here and there in Hamburg as in Berlin two or three are seen haggling in a shop doorway, and cigarettes are seen to change hands; at another time a bigger crowd is seen and higher prices. Sometimes policemen appear; the crowd is forced to disperse, and two or three of the busier traders are escorted away. Officially, the black market is against the law, but this is a pure hypocrisy in that the German police themselves deal abundantly in it. 'How can they be expected to do otherwise?' said an English military officer to me yesterday, 'when their wages are so low and their food so scarce – too scarce to sustain them.'

But – and this is wretched – the prices on the black market are so high that the common worker, who earns on average about 200 reichsmarks a month, cannot trade in it, let alone the destitute, the old, the blind and the solitary. Nor can they live through the third bitter winter that faces them on 1,500-1,700 calories a day. In the official market, the price of a three pound loaf is half a mark; on the black market 50 marks (or ten cigarettes) and more must be paid – a week's wage for a worker. The buying of bread even, without mentioning other foodstuffs, is beyond the reach of hundreds of individuals and very many families. During the last two years they have been forced to exchange their goods, spare clothes, dishes, furniture, and often to hire out themselves, in order to buy the hardly-sufficient-to-live ration. By today they have hardly anything remaining to sell for food, and they are themselves so much weaker after the suffering of two hard winters.

Some hundreds of Berlin inhabitants died last winter: there are various estimates; it is impossible to know which is correct. Every day, in the newspapers, there was a long list, 'died of starvation'; another list, 'died of cold'; and a third list, as long as the first two, of those who had committed suicide.

Next winter there will be more, many more, people dying of starvation and cold in Berlin, as in most of Germany's cities. It is impossible to live through a hard winter on the Continent on just 1,500 calories a day, and as the unreasonable prices of the black market are way beyond their means, what hope have they?

The weak have become weaker, the poor poorer, the old older, the clothes more scarce, and the shoes in many families useless. When the rain and snow and cold arrive, what hope will they have? According to official figures supplied to the Press recently, not one out of three Hamburg inhabitants has any spare underwear; not one out of three of the population has waterproof shoes. Those homes that are in the zone of Berlin under the French jurisdiction received only a hundredweight of coal – during the last two years. Up until now they have not been promised more than 50 pounds of coal for the next winter. Matters are not much better in the other zones. Can you imagine the distress and suffering to come? The majority will survive, others – they have no hope. And presently, the Quakers, the IVSP and the Salvation Army, those organisations who distribute food and clothing amongst the Germans, have to cut back their work because of the decreasing stocks coming from England and America.

If you were but to see the Berlin population today as they walk the streets, with pale and downcast faces, if you were but to see their barefooted children, often walking in the rain with only their skin as cover for their bones, and their young stomachs already beginning to swell, a sign that cruel starvation is threatening. If you were but to stand at one of the Es-Bahn stations of Berlin and see the crowds thronging on their way home with heavy burdens on their backs. They have been out in the country trying to exchange dishes or cigarettes for a few potatoes or vegetables, and are returning home burdened with their loads and pain. You must see them before you can appreciate the situation. Here is a sixty-year-old woman bent double by the load on her back; a young mother in her rags trying to carry three or four packages and keep an eye on her children. An old man who can hardly move because of the weight of the sack he is dragging behind him, and a young girl struggling to push the rickety, loaded wheelbarrow before her.

They all rush into their carriages and then slump either onto their seats or their packs; no smile, no words. Every face full of anxiety and weariness. Any minute, the police may walk in and take away everything. According to the law it is forbidden to carry food from the Russian zone of the countryside around back into the city.

Articles

This morning I visited the home of a young mother who had been out throughout last night attempting to exchange cigarettes for potatoes; she succeeded, but on the way home a policeman had taken the potatoes from her and left her to return home empty-handed. The police officer had a good meal, but the woman did not know where the next meal would come from. I left her with her small child sobbing on her arm.

'No coal, no light, no food...'

It is now August; although only two pounds of vegetables is the official ration in the summer, it is possible to go to the countryside in the hope of bringing something home safely, and the gardens are a great help. How will it be here in the winter, in a few months time, with the rain and wind, without roof, without light, without food, without anything?

Was that the question on the mind of the woman who threw herself under the wheels of the underground train, when I was standing on Alexander Platz Station, Berlin, the other day? Was that the question that forced the boys and young men that I saw in prison last Sunday morning to challenge the law of the land? It is true that the number of crimes carried out by the young is increasing daily, but crime and law-breaking here are just part of the effort to live.

It is exactly the same necessity that is driving young girls on to the streets at night to sell their bodies for a cigarette or two – it may help them to buy a loaf tomorrow!

The father of the ex-prisoner of war whom I mentioned at the beginning was attacked. He lost money and some of his clothes. A young student fell asleep in one of Berlin's stations on her way home after having travelled all night; everything that she had with her disappeared except the clothes that she wore. Can those responsible be blamed in their attempts to keep famine and death at bay?

In Berlin and Hamburg and, most probably, in the other towns of Germany, a generation of young people is being raised with no hope or ideals but only the hope of life if they succeed in deceit and theft, and that is their ideal. Every man for himself, that is the basic principle which is completely necessary under such circumstances. Can anything else be expected?

Today, the people of Germany are blamed for failing to oppose the evil ways of their leaders during the last 15 years. Some day, we too will be condemned, the church especially, for being so cowardly in our judgements and so barren in our efforts and sacrifice on behalf of the hungry and destitute – we pass by 'on the other side'.

Who was responsible for the life of that woman on Alexander Platz Station, the other day? The Germans – 'they have brought this upon themselves, let us leave them to enjoy the consequences'? Was it the authorities presently responsible for administering affairs here in Germany? Or was it those who could help the thousands like that woman, should they wish to, but who cannot be bothered to do so? Who is responsible – yourself?

The German people fear another war
The terror of Russian oppression
You do not have to stay long in Berlin before realising that the population lives in fear. The dancing and the flocking to the few cinemas and theatres that are open, or all the walking in the streets in fashionable clothes – something that is at times shocking as you remember the awful poverty of the majority – this is nothing but a feeble effort to escape anxiety and utter hopelessness.

The physical suffering of the last two years has been intense, but the mental suffering has been no less. Sorrow over what is, fear of what is to come – that is the state of Berlin and the whole of the zone under Russian 'care'.

In addition to the continual anxiety for the next meal – for money to pay the rent, for sufficient clothing at least to hide their nakedness, for there is no hope of sufficient to keep warm, for patience to live together with the three families that share the same part of the house, for the child developing TB, or the husband a prisoner in Russia – there is a worse anxiety for the thousands who are aware of what is happening in this part of the world.

Very few of the people of Berlin today believe that there is any hope for continual peace for Germany. They are convinced by now that the fate of their country has been decided. Either the country will be divided in two, with the western half in the hands of the Allies, and the promise that someday it may return into German hands, and the eastern half in the hands of the Russians and the German Communists; or, very soon, another war will break out, between America and Britain on the one hand and Russia on the other.

Remembering Celt

From *Gorwelion*, the magazine of Llangefni Evangelical Church,
Winter 1998

We stood, not able to speak a word, beside a mound of gorse. A black hearse carrying a coffin on which there were no flowers was moving quietly along the tarmac road from Eryri Hospital, Caernarfon, along the Morfa towards the town. We knew it was carrying the body of a friend to his home in Nefyn to be buried.

There was nothing we could now say or do but retrace our steps to the town and complete our journey on the Saturday morning from Mawddwy to the retreat for Bangor students arranged for the Sunday at Plas-y-nant, Betws Garmon. Yet, before leaving, the conviction that had taken hold of both Mair and myself was that we would have a great deal to do. If Celt [Hughes] had left us, then the two of us had to give ourselves fully, for as long as we could, in seeking to maintain 'the work', or 'the blessing' as we referred to it, that had begun amongst us as students at Bangor and at other colleges in Wales.

It was early in January of 1950. I had agreed with Celt, should he not experience a miraculous recovery from the MS that afflicted him by that Saturday morning, that I would call to write on his behalf to Calfaria Church, Aberdare, informing them that he did not wish them to wait further for him as their minister-elect. It was Celt himself who had suggested this.

One morning, at his suggestion, with a nurse who had been greatly influenced by his witness, I anointed him with oil. But it was not given to us to pray 'the prayer of faith' that morning, nor on the other occasions when Bangor students would meet in the evenings to pray earnestly for his recovery. We would kneel at the same spot at those times. And it was at that spot again that I had the privilege of writing on his behalf to the church at Aberdare, and found myself catching my breath more than once as I marvelled at his quiet, trusting spirit.

A Father in the Faith

I preached twice on his behalf at that church, at times when he could hardly lift a hand, but still hoped that God would answer our prayers. I shall never forget being told by him, shortly before I went down for the last time to preach on his behalf, that he had the texts for me for the two services, morning and evening. 'For my thoughts are not your thoughts, neither are your ways my ways, saith the Lord,' was the first. He succeeded in beginning the second text, 'The Lord reigneth,' but he could not continue. On seeing him failing to get the next words out, I tried to help. 'Let the people tremble,' I said. 'No,' he answered, laughing heartily at my mistake, with his blue eyes shining – 'Let the earth rejoice!'

On the last visit, one of the senior officers of the church explained to me that there was a feeling among the younger generation of the church that it should be suggested to Celt that he withdraw his name as minister-elect as time was passing and the church suffering. If that should happen, he said fearfully, it would split the church. In the providence of God, Celt died suddenly in the night before the letter was written. Unknown to his friends, at least, the disease had attacked his throat and produced an inflammation on his lungs.

I had received a card from the nurse who had been so kind to him, a few days before, telling me that there was no indication of any improvement in his condition and that they would be expecting me on the Saturday. The news was broken to the two of us as we descended from the bus on the *Maes* at Caernarfon, on our way, as we thought, to the hospital to write the letter.

A few days later, we stood beside his coffin in the small parlour of his home at Nefyn listening to his Principal's tribute to him. He was one of the most popular students in the College, a fine footballer, a member of the *Noson Lawen* singing group, and faithful in his support of the SCM. If anyone deserved praise, it was Celt. But his Principal went too far. 'Here is one,' he said, 'who did not need to be reborn.' However, we all knew that Celt, having sought long, had known, before being afflicted by the disease, a spiritual experience that had changed his life completely. I almost expected to see the lid of the coffin rising and Celt himself protesting at such error. It was not true. It cannot be true of any one of us. And Celt would have been the first to say so. Here is the story.

At the beginning of the spring term of 1948, he stood at one of the desks of the lecture-room of the Baptist College in Bangor where a number of students, who had been at a retreat at Plas-y-nant, had decided to meet to describe the events of the weekend. Celt had failed to be present, probably because he had been preaching elsewhere on the Sunday. It had been a most blessed weekend. Having listened to one after another of his friends giving their story, he got up on his feet. 'Well,' he said, as amiable as ever, 'it hasn't happened to me yet, but I'm very hopeful it will happen to me soon.'

It happened that very term. He asked me to call in at his lodgings in College Road, as I was passing by one afternoon, for me to hear of how he had received assurance the previous evening that God had forgiven his sins and that he belonged to Him. A few weeks later, I stood at the table in his room reading, at his request, a piece from the *Reader's Digest* that he had come across. The doctors had explained to him shortly before that he was suffering from MS. This was the cause of the weakness in his knees as he had walked from his seat to the pulpit on the Sunday night that he had received the call, and which he had described to me as 'a man walking on a wire trapeze.'

The article made it cruelly clear that there was no treatment available for such a disease. 'What will you do with Calfaria Church now?' I asked, feeling unable to offer any kind of comfort to him under the circumstances. 'I would love to be able to go there,' he said, 'but if not…'. After a short pause, he said, smiling gently, 'leave it to Him.' The students of Bangor would have made short shrift of any pseudo-piety. No-one had cause to do so with Celt.

His condition deteriorated rapidly. He was at Liverpool Royal Hospital for some time. It was there that I had the strange experience of being taken to his bedside by a young nurse who turned around suddenly as I followed her, and said, rather fiercely it seemed, 'That boy! He's got something I haven't got.' She was not the last to say so, especially after he had been transferred to the C&A Hospital, Bangor, and his condition deteriorated to such an extent that he had to be helped to eat. Even then, if you dared pull his leg, his teasing response would always be, 'Once I get mad…'. And he unable to unclasp his hand, let alone lift an arm!

The students who were at his bedside regularly would help him with his meals. Now and again he would send me to others in the ward with whom he had had a conversation. Once I was sent to a man who had been touched to the core on reading the verse, 'Therefore if any man be in Christ, he is a new creature: old things are passed away; behold all things are become new,' which was the 'verse for the day' in one of the London papers. It was that, and the fact that he had had quite a few 'good conversations' with Celt, that convinced the two of us that he had died a Christian. Afterwards we heard that it was 'people from the clubs' – who were considerably less acceptable to the general public then than they are by now – who were at his funeral.

But the time that will always remain in my memory is the afternoon that I called on Celt when his Bible class was in progress. I had never before, nor have since, seen anything like it. Celt was seated in his chair between two beds with his Bible open before him, not able to move hand or foot and having great difficulty in speaking. Slowly his pupils would collect either side of him on the two beds, with myself by now amongst them. As we waited to begin – though I had no idea what was going to happen, remembering the limitations of the teacher – I saw, at the far end of the ward, a group of young men who had been playing cards stopping their game quietly and returning to their beds.

Celt's method of leading his class was by asking questions initially, doing so only through great effort and with the help of one or two others who were most familiar with the subject, and then allowing all to contribute. Then, with a smile or a frown, his raised eyebrows or a shake of his head, he would lead the discussion. He could scarcely contribute further because of the effort required. In my folly, on the one occasion when I joined his 'class', I tried to give a prod to the discussion now and again. I soon realised that I was taking Celt's place, and with a sense of release and wonder I asked to be excused.

Nearly fifty years have passed since losing Celt. Many times, in the meantime, when standing at the graveside of those like himself who have been taken from us much sooner than we would wish, and on considering what they might have achieved for the Kingdom, the question has been asked, Why? We will not be given an answer this side of the grave but we will receive it one day. And the conclusion at that time, certainly, will be that God did all things well.

In the meantime, our place is to be thankful for having known them and from having benefitted so much ourselves from being allowed to labour together with them in the work of the Kingdom.

Articles

Memories of Blaenau

(From the papers of J. Elwyn Davies. The article was intended for a booklet celebrating the hundredth anniversary of Jerusalem Congregational Church, Blaenau Ffestiniog, in 1969 but the booklet was never published. Anniversary services were held.)

It is a difficult task to write about those matters that lie closest to a man's heart. At the most sacred moments of life we are left short of words if not dumb. That is how I feel as I try to gather these few words for the celebration booklet. A hundred times since I was the minister of Jerusalem, my mind has flown back there and my spirit has re-lived the lovely and sacred experiences that we enjoyed during those years. It is a much more difficult task to seek to gather and impart the enchantment of those memories within the bounds of these brief lines.

When I became a minister in Blaenau, I would get the same story from all the inhabitants that I met, 'Blaenau will grow on you – the longer you stay here, the harder it will be for you to think of leaving.' I heard this said so often and so definitely that I had come to believe it firmly before the end of my first year there. But after two or three years, I did not believe it because of having heard it so often but because it was true. I know that I will be thankful throughout my life that the path of grace and of God's providence led me to the church at Jerusalem as the place where a pastoral charge, and the fine responsibility of preaching the gospel, was first laid upon me. On looking back, I feel certain that there was no better or more appropriate place in Wales for a minister, holding to those principles that had been planted in me in college days, to begin his career.

I well remember, after hearing of the call to the church, that I visited the late Principal Gwilym Bowyer and told him that I feared the responsibility of a church with so many members. 'No,' he said, 'the fact that you are young and lacking in experience will be in your favour. The church will be that much more ready to sympathise with your efforts, and to forgive also.' He spoke a true word, and my gratitude to the church is deep indeed.

During my years of ministry in Jerusalem I came to appreciate one aspect of the life of the church more than almost any other, namely the effort made at all times – particularly on the part of the deacons – to administer and direct the life of the church in the most dignified and courteous way. Though the bareness of the hills and the craggy ruggedness of the mountains were of the essence of the place, and though the inhabitants, like their environment, were unostentatious, open and without flattery towards one another, yet, in the life of the church, the respect for God was evident and the living sense of a responsibility towards a locality leavened every conversation and sobered the roughest. It was not just once or twice, as the familiar are aware, that the former secretary would plead for the express protection of heaven, arguing that Jerusalem was like a city set upon a hill that could not be hid. Another officer confessed with tears,

> Ni allaf roddi fel y rhoddaist im;
> 'Rwy'n gweld, yng ngolau'r groes, fy ngorau'n ddim.

> I cannot give as thou hast given me;
> My best is nothing, seen at Calvary.

Directness of speech, sincerity and spiritual dignity: the savour of these characteristics still remain clearly in my mind today – characteristics that were equally as present in the small vestry meetings as in the more numerous services of the chapel.

One of the main features of Welsh nonconformity in the past was the great emphasis placed on preaching the gospel. Although this tradition is quickly declining in present-day Wales, it was respected at Jerusalem. And to ascend the pulpit stairs to break open the bread of life, Sunday by Sunday, was a very sacred experience. It was not for no purpose that the pulpit was placed centrally in our places of worship and that priority was given to preaching. When we consider the great Subject and his message, an awesome responsibility rests on the messenger – a responsibility that forces the most loyal and brave, bearing in mind the opportunities given, to acknowledge that we have been unprofitable servants so many times. A great responsibility rests also on the shoulders of the church that she seeks constantly for herself and her messenger the divine anointing upon the preaching of the Word that will provide meaning and spiritual charge to the truth. I will not forget the discussions of the *seiat* nor the fervent prayers in the young people's prayer meeting on a Sunday afternoon and in the mid-week meetings. From age to age the old man changes and falls into oblivion. It is the divine seed and the fruit that counts. With a sincere heart I am thankful for serving my apprenticeship in the Jerusalem pulpit and at the square table with its Bible in the small vestry.

As in the experience of every minister who undertakes the care of a church, there already existed a pattern of weekly meetings at Jerusalem, and each one had good support on the whole. There were only very few members who were not associated with some aspect or other of the life of the church in its weekly activities. Bearing in mind the grievous decline that has occurred in recent years, we can but be thankful for such a pattern and tradition. I am grateful for those parents who came to support their children in the Band of Hope – not one row, but often two or three. The small vestry was often fairly full for a *seiat* or prayer meeting. And evident also was the wonderful loyalty of the members of the literary society with its programme which was as tasteful and edifying as possible. But 'the wind bloweth where it listeth', and we mortals must be flexible and humble enough in spirit to remember this. Some of the children of the church began to meet together of their own accord on Friday evenings. There was given to them a missionary zeal greater than was to be seen in any other aspect of the church. As a result, the small circle of 'children of the reception class' grew into a strong troop of local children. They met together, they pastored each other. Before every meeting, whether a talk or a Bible study, they held their own prayer meeting with the majority of them taking part. It came from heaven, ever the source of quickening life. It came about, it came to an end, but its fruit remains today in the consecrated and mission-minded lives of many of the church's children. It was no flash in the pan, nor yet the fruit of natural effort. A breeze from heaven passed by – and as one who had the privilege of being present, I now know what I believed then, that in the pure, unpolluted breath of those same Divine breezes lies the hope of the continuation of the gospel's witness in our land.

A Father in the Faith

I could not close these remarks without adding one further word of thanks to the members of Jerusalem for the privilege of entering their homes, and entering also into the private and sacred world of their experiences and trials, the bitter and the sweet together, during my years amongst them. It was a great privilege to receive such kindness and such trust within the homes of the church. We will never forget those years because, in the light of them, the two of us succeeded in raising our first home and learning how to live. May the smiles of heaven fall abundantly on every home amongst you and the Divine arm protect you from all evil.

Religion by now is confronted by days of severe testing. We now see that the days of Welsh nonconformist religion, as we received it in the first half of the century, are numbered. Without doubt, great and inevitable changes lie on the horizon. O that the strong winds would blow once more, driving whole districts to their knees and raising churches full of fire and zeal for God and his amazing love in the Lord Jesus Christ. I cannot wish more for Jerusalem than to pray that God would use them for this purpose.

Unwitting backsliders

From *The Evangelical Magazine of Wales*, Autumn/Winter 1956-57

Anyone who thinks seriously about the condition of our country at the present time cannot but become more and more convinced that nothing but a true re-awakening from above can deal effectively with the present situation. When a man becomes thus convinced, he cannot, if he be a child of God, fail to yearn that such a visitation might come about, and that soon. Two factors account for this. On the one hand, he is possessed of a desire that God's name might be glorified and honoured. This, he realises, takes place pre-eminently during every time of revival. On the other hand, he desires to see men and women in ever-increasing numbers coming to a personal knowledge of the One who is *his* Saviour and Lord. He realises that this too occurs on a very wide scale during a revival. Consequently, he cannot but pray to that end.

Yet, although the times testify clearly that it is the duty of every true Christian to be on his knees, fervently praying for revival, it is still possible for the believer himself to be so cold of heart and lacking in zeal as to be totally indifferent and apathetic. His love towards God has grown cold and he therefore knows no sorrow as he contemplates the way in which God's name is ignored and debased in our day. His love towards his fellow-men has correspondingly diminished, and he neither sheds a tear nor loses a moment's sleep at the thought of the multitudes around him who, unless there be a visitation from on high in our own day, must face life and eternity without God and without hope.

How easy it is to drift into coldness of spirit and hardness of heart! Although it may be difficult to believe, much less to acknowledge, it is nevertheless a fact that one can remain in this state for months, or even years, *without realising it*. Indeed, in one sense, the last charge that could be levelled against us at such a time is that we have drifted away from God. We read our Bibles, we pray, we appear to be full of zeal for the affairs of the Kingdom, but one thing of fundamental importance is lacking. Even though we do not neglect the Bible (we read it) or prayer (we practise it) or service (we perform it) *we are guilty of neglecting God Himself.* It is possible to pray and to read the Word and to serve, and yet to allow our fellowship with God to languish.

Let us test ourselves. The Christian who communes daily with God cannot fail to love Him, nor can he consequently fail to love his fellows. Let us apply the first test to our own lives. Do you love God *with all your heart, with all your soul, with all your strength?* The love of those who give priority to their fellowship with God over all else in their lives is a love of that quality. They live in an awareness of God; and their love towards Him is a minute-to-minute reality. Do you and I know anything at all of such a love as *this?* It may well be that we knew something of it in those early days of our spiritual pilgrimage, but is it equally true (indeed it should be more true) of us today? Or is our love spasmodic, flickering, and feeble in its influence? Notwithstanding our undisputed fervour in prayer and sincerity in worship, we know that the pulsating thrill which once governed our lives is lost.

Let us apply to ourselves the second test. Another inevitable characteristic of a Christian who lives in the presence of God is an ever-increasing love towards his fellow-men. We would do well to read some of the biographies of saints of former days to see the warmth that characterised their prayers, the utterness of their care for one soul, and the incredible self-sacrifice that was characteristic of their religious life. Late into the night they would pray for a service, *and no one would hear mention of it;* they fasted regularly, they laboured unsparingly – and all because of their all-consuming love for God and their sincere love for man. Do you and I know ought of this love? It is possible that in the early days of our Christian life we knew it, and that in the rousing events of an evangelistic campaign we taste it afresh; *but are we such people?*

We have lost the thrill, the vibrant thrill of love. How has this come about? There is only one explanation. *We are guilty of neglecting our fellowship with God and with His Son Jesus Christ.* No, it is not a matter of committing petty sins, though these can certainly be the occasion of the diminishing of our love and the hiding of His face from us. As we know full well, guilt should not separate us from Him for a single moment. We know that there is forgiveness. The basic sin is that of neglecting God, and the fundamental charge which we must answer is that *we are willing to be enticed and estranged from God.*

Christians today can be divided into three groups (not two, as we often think – namely, those who have fallen away from God and those who persevere in the faith – but three). First of all, we must acknowledge the existence of that large group of believers, who, in this age as in every other, have apparently renounced their faith and have returned to the world. To this class we could give the title of *open* backsliders; believers and yet backsliders. Then there is another class of backsliders, the *unwitting* backsliders. Outwardly those who belong to this group are above criticism, but for all that, when they are compared with the third group, it becomes quite evident that they too are backsliders. *They too are people who have wandered away from God*. They have kept the externals of their religion, and by that we mean the reading of Scriptures, prayer, witnessing, tithing and regular attendance at meetings. The reality of their conversion cannot for a moment be doubted; they are children of God; *but they have wandered away from Him*.

To see this clearly, shall we compare them – and ourselves also – with members of the third group? The members of this group put God first. At this point, members of the second group will immediately protest and argue that they too do that, but let us pause for a moment to consider. Neither pressure of work, nor the demands of the day, nor evangelistic activity, *nor any other thing*, can cause the believers of the third group to neglect the hour of prayer. Whatever else may suffer, as duties and responsibilities multiply, they always take care to allow at least as much, if not more time to God than they did previously. *They put God Himself first.*

Furthermore, there are two most important features to this hour of prayer. In the first place, it may easily be an hour, or indeed even longer. Let no one shake his head by way of protest or doubt: this has been literally true of those people who have done most for God in every age. They put God *Himself* first. The second feature of this hour of prayer is this. God Himself is given the first place *in it*. They pray as Jesus Christ taught His disciples to pray, putting the things of God first: His name, His Kingdom, His will, and their own needs last of all.

And what of the 'hour of prayer' itself? As we have previously acknowledged, the members of this second group *do* pray. But the first complaint that must be made against them is this: an 'hour of prayer' is hardly ever a true description of their devotions. They pray just as they would write a letter. 'Dear Father, which art in heaven,' they say, and immediately they set about making a list of their wants. That being done, they proceed with the tasks of the day, rejoicing in the fact that the letter (i.e. their prayers) has been sent. They hurry into the Presence, are hurried in their prayers, and are in just as much of a hurry to get up from their knees after praying. *In a word, there is good reason for doubting whether they know anything at all about prayer.* Prayer, by its very nature and purpose, is fellowship with God. The testimony of His saints down through the centuries is this. In the first place, they are at pains to assure us that it takes time – quite literally – for people like ourselves, particularly when we are novices in these matters, to enter into God's presence; and that even when we have arrived *there*, it requires an effort on our part – again, quite literally – to remain there. Then, secondly, they assure us that prayer on this level is altogether different from the asking-for-things-only kind of prayer. *It does not belong to the same world.*

How much, one wonders, do we know about *this*? Do we know what it is to linger silently but deliberately before the Throne of Grace until such time as we find ourselves, through the Spirit, in His presence, and what it is to tarry there when the world and the flesh and the devil would conspire desperately to drag us to our feet? Or do we rather yield to the insistent temptation to arise from our knees unblessed? If such be our experience, let us confess it, and let us desire with a sense of compelling urgency to give this absolute priority in our spiritual lives – that we will seek God Himself until we find him; that we will do so daily; that we will refuse to get up from our knees unless we have beheld his face.

Another characteristic of our prayers in this period of declension is, that we tend to think of ourselves, first and last. We *ask* for guidance, we *pray* for ease of mind or peace of conscience. It is not God we seek, but the benefits He bestows. We turn to Him to seek these blessings and favours, and having presented our petitions, we go away. Not without reason did the Lord Jesus Christ, in His prayer, relegate petitions for forgiveness, for daily bread and for deliverance from evil to the fourth, fifth and sixth petitions respectively. May God pardon us if, after a glib salutation, we rush past the first three petitions, and ask only for these favours for ourselves. It was not without reason, indeed, that the Lord Jesus bade us first of all to address God and to address Him as Father: if only we did that meaningfully, the other petitions would follow naturally *and in their right order.*

Are we to be found today among those of the second group, the unwitting backsliders? Unknowingly, we have slipped into contenting ourselves with a religion whose centre is not God Himself. It is relatively little of our time that we devote to Him, that we might have fellowship with Him in His Word and in prayer. Unwittingly we have become accustomed to, and satisfied with, this state of affairs. And yet in our heart of hearts, we know that something vital is missing – we do not enjoy the Word, we know nothing of victory over sin, our testimony has lost the eagerness and spontaneity of former days, we experience no blessing when we pray. Unwittingly, we said, and in a sense that is true; and yet, we are well aware of it, we simply will not confess it and face up to it. And the root cause of the degeneration, as we have seen, is our neglect of God Himself.

Let us then return to God and let us give ourselves completely to Him – not to His service, initially, but to God Himself and to His fellowship. Service will follow inevitably. Let us resolutely seek to subordinate all else to our relationship to Him, then we shall find that our spiritual life will be renewed in every part. Our love for Him will revive, as will also our love towards our fellows. We will not argue for that love, we ourselves will be living witnesses of it. We will find ourselves desiring the glory of God's name. It will become an all-consuming passion. We shall long to see men and women partaking of the blessing which we have known, and our longing will become a veritable travail of spirit. We shall love God with all our mind, heart and strength, and our neighbour as ourselves; our life will be governed yet again by the thrill and vibrancy of former days. We shall pray for revival – we will find ourselves having to do so – and we shall find that great and precious promises are given to us. 'If My people which are called by My name shall humble themselves, and pray, and seek My face, and turn from their wicked ways; then I will hear from heaven and will forgive their sin, and will heal their land' (2 Chronicles 7:14).

God's gift to a nation

From *The Evangelical Magazine of Wales*, April 1981

The task of attempting so soon after his passing a brief assessment of Dr Lloyd-Jones' ministry, and in particular of his influence on church life in Wales, is well-nigh an impossible one. The impact of his life and ministry, extending over more than half a century, has been so profound that one is truly at a loss to know where to begin. The words of the Welsh hymn, sung with such fervour by the company of relatives and friends who were gathered around his grave at Newcastle Emlyn, say it all. It is from the vantage point of 'heavenly Jerusalem's towers' alone that we shall be able with any measure of certainty to trace the path along which we have been led through 'the desert' of life.

To attempt to do this is incumbent upon us, however, if only to enable us to return thanks to God for all that he achieved through the ministry of His servant.

And we would be doing a gross injustice to that story if we failed to start with his remarkable period of ministry at Sandfields, Aberavon. In a very real sense the eleven years he spent there served to shape and to determine his lifelong convictions. His subsequent ministry at Westminster Chapel with its world-wide ramifications – through the publication of his sermons and the many thousands of foreign students and others who worshipped there over the years – could so easily dazzle our eyes to the remarkable years of his first period of ministry. Most certainly, no account of his impact and influence on the Welsh religious scene could ignore this formative period in his life.

No one who knew Dr Lloyd-Jones would be left in any uncertainty as to his love for Wales and for its people. Thus, when he felt called to leave the field of medicine and to devote his life to the work of the ministry, it seemed right to him that he should offer his services to the Forward Movement of the Presbyterian Church of Wales. But there was a further reason why he chose to do this. In a television interview with the late Aneirin Talfan Davies he once explained that his father's radical views and his concerns for the poor and underprivileged had had a profound effect upon him. This was why he was particularly anxious to minister in the kind of areas that were then being served by the Forward Movement.

That the hand of God was upon him, inclining him in the direction that was eventually to bring him to the church at Sandfields, Aberavon, was made evident by the many tokens of blessing and favour that attended his labours there. From the working-class community of that town and neighbourhood, through his anointed labours, God called and redeemed many remarkable trophies of grace. Soon a sizeable congregation of men was to gather regularly on a Saturday evening to attend the Doctor's 'brotherhood discussion session'. And before he left, eleven years later, the congregation had grown to such proportions that an annexe had to be built alongside the church building, enabling the overflowing numbers to follow the services through the open windows of the chapel.

News of Dr Lloyd-Jones' call to the ministry and the fame of his preaching spread far and wide, and it was from that town, so strategically placed in south Wales, that God sent His servant, in what became a regular mid-week ministry, bearing the message of salvation to all parts of Wales and beyond. It may be difficult for us today to imagine what it was like. Those were days when, in Wales at least, the chapels were full, and the entire population, it seemed, was in membership in some chapel or other. To a young lad in his early teens at the time it also seemed as though everyone went to hear the Doctor, wherever he preached.

Looking back over those years, Dr Lloyd-Jones was well aware that there were Christians in Wales at that time who were disappointed that he had felt unable to identify himself wholeheartedly with their testimony. And it is true to say that the Doctor himself could not fully explain at the time why it was that he could not bring himself to be associated with, for example, some of the Pentecostal and Keswick traditions which had emerged in Wales following the '04-'05 Revival.

These were years when he was possessed with one consuming passion – to tell men that in and through the Lord Jesus Christ they could know God. They were also the years when for the first time, following upon his distinguished medical career, he was able to give himself avidly to the study of theology and Christian doctrine. There is the famous story of how he was challenged at the close of a service in Bridgend by a minister who commented provocatively, 'I cannot make up my mind what you are. I cannot decide whether you are a hyper-Calvinist or a Quaker.' On being asked why the comment was being made, he was told, 'You talk of God's action and God's sovereignty like a hyper-Calvinist and of spiritual experience like a Quaker, but the Cross and the work of Christ have very little place in your preaching.' Assuring him that he was not a hyper-Calvinist, the Doctor's response was to ask the Rev. Vernon Lewis – later to be made Principal of the Memorial (Congregational) College at Brecon – when he called the following Monday morning, what he could read on the Atonement. He was referred to the works of P. T. Forsyth, R. W. Dale's *The Atonement*, and Denney's *The Death of Christ* – such was the dearth of truly evangelical literature at the time.

Commenting on this incident in later years, the Doctor explained that in his early preaching he was like Whitefield. First and foremost he preached regeneration: man's own efforts were useless; he needed power from outside himself. 'I assumed the atonement but did not distinctly preach it or justification by faith.'

A little later, in a second-hand bookshop in Cardiff he came across the two-volume edition of the works of Jonathan Edwards, and later still to his great delight on a visit to the United States, the entire works of Warfield. Years afterwards the Doctor was to explain that what kept him from identifying himself with the traditions to which we have referred was his knowledge of what God had done in the past through men like Daniel Rowland of Llangeitho, Howell Harris and others. He was looking for those who shared their view of doctrine, but, more, their view of experimental religion and of revival.

And such people were at a premium in the denomination to which he was attached, as they had once been. To us today it seems so regrettable that Dr Lloyd-Jones was ordained a minister of the Presbyterian Church of Wales when it was too late even for a person of his gifts and convictions to influence the issue of whether the denomination should adopt a Shorter Confession, and thus to all intents and purposes, relegate the old Confession of Faith to the status of a historical document. Such was the case, however, and even though at one time Dr Lloyd-Jones had reason to hope that the common people, in response to his preaching, would reject the arrogant views of the vast majority of liberal and modernist preachers who by then were occupying the pulpits of our land, this was not to be.

On one occasion he was given what seemed to him a most promising portent for good. He had been invited to preach in the same Association meeting as the Rev. Tom Nefyn Williams, probably the most radical of all the liberal preachers of the day, a man of considerable talent and charm. The Doctor would recount the story of how he came down to breakfast on that occasion, only to sense as soon as he entered the room that an uncomfortable silence had fallen upon all those who were at the tables. Upon making discreet enquiry, he was asked chidingly, 'Don't you know what's happening? They are all debating who will get the biggest congregation, Tom Nefyn or yourself.' At the first of the two services at which they were to preach, each man's congregation had been more or less equal. But at this first service Dr Lloyd-Jones had been given remarkable liberty in preaching, so that by the second service his meeting was full to overflowing, while the Rev. Tom Nefyn's congregation had been considerably reduced.

But it was not to be. A few years later Dr Lloyd-Jones was given incontrovertible proof that if the common people were prepared to hear him gladly, a good number of the religious leaders of his denomination had been considerably irked by his uncompromising adherence to the evangelical faith. They were prepared to resist quite openly a proposal which, if accepted, could have meant his sphere of influence within the denomination being considerably enhanced. After eleven years of intensive work at Port Talbot, it was suggested that he be appointed, in a year's time, to the staff of the Theological College of the Presbyterian Church of Wales at Bala, under the Rev. David Phillips as Principal. Although the proposal was favoured by the Associations in the south and east, the North Wales Association kept deferring a decision – a deliberate ploy, on the part of some of the leaders at least, to avoid the opprobrium of an outright rejection, whilst at the same time making it obvious to the Doctor and others that his services were not welcome.

In the meantime, while his own heart was very much inclined towards the Bala vacancy, Dr Lloyd-Jones had been invited to assist Dr Campbell Morgan at Westminster Chapel. Within six weeks of his going there he had been invited to continue on a permanent basis. But from October

1938 until after Easter 1939 he refused to commit himself, still waiting for a firm invitation to the College at Bala – an invitation which never came. The Doctor had persuaded the friends at Westminster Chapel to await the decision of the North Wales Association's meetings to be held at Chester. Three ministers had fully intended going to those meetings and pressing for a favourable response, but for different reasons all three were unable to be present, and the matter was once again left on the table. The Doctor had no alternative but to accept the invitation to become co-pastor with Dr Campbell Morgan and thus to commence his 35 years of ministry at Westminster Chapel.

As is so often said on such occasions, 'Wales's loss was surely England's gain.' In the hindsight of close on half a century we now know that that step, which to some might have seemed so regrettable at the time, proved to be possibly the most far-reaching and consequential development this century in the history of the evangelical cause in Britain, if not throughout the world. However influential the Doctor's ministry might have been in a finishing college devoted primarily to pastoralia, how can one begin to compute the influence for good of this prince among preachers, this wise counsellor and spiritual leader, through his pulpit ministry, his Friday evening lectures, his meetings for ministers, the Westminster Conferences, his wider preaching ministry, his availability at all times for counsel and advice – a ministry which is to continue through his printed works and through the kind providence that has enabled his spoken word to be preserved, so that to an uncanny degree we are able to hear the Doctor as though he were yet with us? All these things, we now know, hinged upon his ministry at Westminster Chapel. We can only say with the Apostle, 'How unsearchable are his judgements, and his ways past finding out!' (Romans 11:33).

It proved to be Wales' gain also, despite the fact that after the 1939-45 war, when it was evident that Nonconformity was losing its grip on the people, Dr Lloyd-Jones would occasionally be criticized for forsaking Wales in its hour of need. One writer even suggested that he had done so for a more lucrative and comfortable ministry in a big church in London! Nothing, of course, could be further from the truth. He never lost touch with the situation in Wales, nor did he show any sign of rancour or bitterness as a result of what had happened. He continued to preach to vast congregations in many centres in Wales. In 1977, for example, he celebrated his fiftieth consecutive annual visit to preach at

Carmarthen. There were many similar instances. His sermons too had a wide circulation.

But it was in the years after the war that his links with Wales assumed a completely different role and significance. Prior to this, his ministry had been that of a visiting preacher, preaching to vast congregations. Now it assumed more that of a friend and counsellor to a body of young men whose labours were eventually to lead to the emergence of faithful evangelical ministries in churches of all denominations in Wales; to the emergence also of what became known – on the Doctor's own suggestion at the Annual Welsh Conference, held in Denbigh in 1955 – as 'The Evangelical Movement of Wales', and later, to the establishing of avowedly evangelical causes free of all denominational entanglements.

The Doctor's interest was first alerted to a movement of the Spirit that occurred in the Colleges of Wales in the years 1945-50. It seemed to have two focal points – one in the south, which because of a strong Presbyterian background was more doctrinal in its thrust, and one in the north, which had a more experimental emphasis. In the providence of God, Dr Lloyd-Jones was brought into very close touch with both streams at the very outset and, in ways which today we can see were graciously ordained of God, was able to assert from the beginning a most salutary, formative and unifying influence.

As a consequence of his remarkable preaching ministry at Westminster Chapel, he had by now been greatly used by the UCCF (or the IVF as it was then known). In his own words, 'I became the theologian of the IVF.' When it was suggested that the work in the recently reinvigorated Welsh Christian Unions would benefit from meeting together in an annual conference, Dr Lloyd-Jones was the obvious choice as speaker. For the first three years he took the main conference addresses, each year taking one major tenet of the Christian faith as his theme. His ministry had a profound effect on the students. One student, who later succeeded to his pulpit at Sandfields, Aberavon – the late Rev. J. B. E. Thomas – would often remark that he had learned more of Christian theology in those conferences than in all the lectures he had ever attended at his Theological College.

No sooner had the blessing broken out in the north than Dr Lloyd-Jones was to speak at a student mission at the University College, Bangor.

There he learned with immense satisfaction of the spontaneous work of the Spirit among the students. Later he was to give his full endorsement to an experience of the further enduement of the Spirit which some of the students had known – an endorsement which coincided with his own renewed interest in the subject of the sealing of the Spirit and revival.

When some of these students came to realise a little later that there was not a single publication in the Welsh language committed to the evangelical faith, Dr Lloyd-Jones was asked to write in the first issue of a new Welsh-language magazine which they published. When, later, they decided to invite the leadership of the magazine to a conference, his daughter Elizabeth attended the first, held at Bala in 1951, and Dr Lloyd-Jones was the main speaker at the second, held at Caernarfon the following year. When, a little later, the need was felt for an equivalent provision in English, Dr Lloyd-Jones was once again the main speaker, returning, to the delight of his many friends, to his pulpit at Sandfields, Aberavon. When some of the students from both north and south Wales were to attend the National Eisteddfod for the first time to sell the new Welsh-language magazine and to witness to their people, Dr Lloyd-Jones met them twice and addressed a late-evening gathering in one of the local churches.

Finally, when some of those students had themselves become ministers, Dr Lloyd-Jones was able to offer invaluable advice which led to the emergence both of the Ministers' Fellowships associated with the Evangelical Movement of Wales and also of its Annual Ministers' Conference. Barring periods of ill-health, the Doctor attended that conference without fail, and every year would lead the two discussion sessions and deliver his memorable closing addresses. Had Dr Lloyd-Jones not been with us at that time, there is little doubt that the work of the gospel in Wales would have taken a very different form.

Some of the evangelical ministers in south Wales were anxious to meet in a monthly ministers' fellowship restricted to brethren of a reformed persuasion. They were anxious to invite the Doctor to the first of what would become an annual gathering of ministers of the same persuasion from all parts of Wales. Dr Lloyd-Jones agreed to be present on condition that they widened the basis of their fellowship – a step which was to lead to incalculable gain and benefit to the cause of the gospel in Wales, and of the reformed faith in particular.

And so the story continued. Throughout the 30 years that followed, the Doctor's interest and support were unfailingly available to all who sought his counsel; his presence and ministry were a source of strength and encouragement to all who knew him. Indeed, so intimately involved was he in the ongoing situation in Wales that for many months, if not years, it will be extremely difficult to accept the fact that he is no longer with us.

Our comfort is surely that of the pastor's wife who, as she glanced at the congregation that sang the hymn at his graveside on March 6th, suddenly noticed how many ministers were present. Dr Lloyd-Jones had been pastor and friend to them all. With the support and constant encouragement of his dear wife and partner Mrs Lloyd-Jones, he had, while physical strength remained, preached in their pulpits and attended all their conferences. In him the words of our Lord had been gloriously fulfilled: 'Whosoever will be great among you, let him be your minister; and whosoever will be chief among you, let him be your servant.' In many things he excelled, but in this most of all.

Wales had never lost one of her ablest sons. Allowed to function freely in a church unfettered by any element of compromise or apostasy, he had continued to serve his people. And now, taken to be with the Lord on St David's Day, 1981, he had come home again, to rest awhile – till He come.

The secret of her strength

From Y *Cylchgrawn Efengylaidd,* August/October 1989. The substance of a sermon preached at the foundation services of Carmarthen Evangelical Church, 25 March 1989.

Strangely enough, the word 'church' appears only twice in the gospels, and both times from the lips of the Lord Jesus Christ himself. What he discloses about his church, however, in the context of these two occasions is of great importance. We refer to Matthew's Gospel, 16:18, 'And I say also unto thee, that thou art Peter, and upon this rock I will build my church', and his further words, in the same gospel, 'And if he shall neglect to hear them, tell it unto the church' (Matthew 18:17).

It will be necessary for us to concentrate our attention on the first key use of the word at Caesarea Philippi. By doing this, however, we shall soon realise that there is a direct connection between the first use and the context of the second.

The best way to deal with the words of the Lord Jesus in Matthew 16:18 is by attempting to answer two questions: (1) Who or what is the rock upon which he builds his church? (2) What does he mean when he says that he will build his church upon this rock? It is one thing to have a rock; it is another thing, it seems, to build a church upon that rock. It must be acknowledged, as we seek answers to these questions, that his strong but responsible words – 'and the gates of hell shall not prevail against it' – will always be in mind. In the Wales of today, there is no-one possessing greater privilege than those who are members of this church and who have proved the secret of her strength.

(1) Who or what, therefore, is intended by 'this rock'?
There is no need to remind anyone that there have been great arguments over the significance of this phrase throughout the centuries. Some have insisted – and still do today – that Peter himself is the rock. But not Peter

alone either, but Peter together with the continuous stream of his direct successors appointed by a college of cardinals in Rome.

No-one would deny for a moment that Peter has an important place in the history of the establishing of the early church, but the Lord Jesus Christ could hardly have wished anyone to believe that his church was to rest entirely on a mortal man, however influential that man's ministry might have been at the beginning. And with respect to his succession, a few minutes after these words had been uttered the first and greatest in this glorious succession was a public spokesman for Satan himself (Matt. 16:23)! And he was not the last such in that succession, as history proves.

Others argue that it is not Peter himself who is the rock, but Peter's confession. And again no-one needs to be reminded that this interpretation is much closer to the tradition in which we have been raised. But we can hardly be satisfied with it. The devil believes, says the Scriptures, and trembles. And there have been thousands of people in Wales, in years past, who have been very ready to maintain this confession, as a bare belief, without the living, dynamic, divinely-inspired spark that characterised Peter's experience being true in their lives. Indeed, as it becomes more popular to profess orthodoxy in the days of the setting of liberalism, the same thing may occur again in Great Britain and in Wales, as it has certainly occurred already in the United States. There are plenty of people to be found today, as there have always been, who are very loath to face the difficult task of winnowing the false from the true – a task that our nonconformist fathers faced manfully and to the great benefit of the church of Jesus Christ and to our nation in the past. It was not for nothing that the Lord Jesus pressed upon his disciples to watch out for false professors.

No, we must dig deeper and examine more carefully these words of Jesus Christ. And if we do so we will notice that there are three important elements to be seen in his description of what had happened in Peter's life. There is here:

Firstly, a meeting between two people, and two greetings given – Peter addresses Jesus Christ, 'Thou art the Christ, the Son of the living God', and the Lord Jesus Christ addresses Peter, 'Blessed art thou, Simon Barjona.'

Secondly, divine activity, an activity that preceded and was responsible for the confession.

Thirdly, a divine attestation that follows and confirms the confession, 'Blessed art thou, Simon Barjona: for flesh and blood hath not revealed it unto thee, but my Father which is in heaven.'

Without taking all these elements into consideration, we shall never do justice to 'the rock' that was in the mind of Jesus Christ when he looked at Peter and greeted him. And that is why it would be more correct to say that it is not Peter's confession that is the Rock, but *Peter's recognition of the Lord Jesus Christ* – a recognition for which the Father was responsible, and the Lord Jesus Christ, therefore, was able to confirm.

At the end of his ministry the Lord Jesus placed these elements concisely together as he addressed his heavenly Father in prayer. He was speaking of that which he and the Father had together fulfilled, not only in Peter's life, but in the lives of all the disciples: 'I have manifested thy name unto the men which thou gavest me out of the world; thine they were, and thou gavest them to me; and they have kept thy word. Now they have known that all things whatsoever thou hast given me are of thee. For I have given unto them the words which thou gavest me; and they have received them, and have known surely that I came out from thee, and they have believed that thou hast sent me' (John:17 6-8). This is the rock upon which the Lord Jesus Christ builds his church. And the great comfort to all, throughout the ages, who in consequence are incorporated into that rock, is that not all the powers of hell can pull down the church that is built upon it. This brings us to our second question.

(2) What does Jesus Christ mean when he says that he will build his church upon this rock?
A rock does not make a church. The rock is necessary, but before there is a church there must be something else also. 'Upon this rock I will build my church.' The church is something that Jesus Christ will build upon this rock – and only upon this rock. To what activity of his is Christ referring? We have the answer in the next verse. In order to weigh his words carefully, we shall divide the verse into two parts. The answer to the question is implied in the first part of the verse; and to those who have eyes to see, it is evident in the second part.

(a) *'And I will give unto thee the keys of the kingdom of heaven.'*
What occasion in Peter's later life was in Christ's mind when he made this extraordinary promise? He was referring to the great privilege that would be given to the apostle on the Day of Pentecost of preaching the gospel for the first time, or, to keep to Christ's symbolism, of making use of 'the keys of the kingdom of heaven' for the first time, and thereby opening wide the doors of that kingdom to all who responded. But notice who it is who will arrange all this. Who is it who will extend to him the privilege and fulfil such a prophecy? 'I will give unto thee,' says Jesus Christ. He did not hand them over to him at that instant, but 'I shall be there to give them to you when the hour arrives.' And he was; he never broke his word to anyone. 'He hath shed forth this, which ye now see and hear' was Peter's own explanation. Let us turn to the second promise.

(b) *'And whatsoever thou shalt bind on earth shall be bound in heaven: and whatsoever thou shalt loose on earth shall be loosed in heaven.'*
At first sight, it seems that Jesus Christ is prophesying that some unique, extraordinary power is to characterise Peter, feeble man, on his own. Moreover, it seems also that Jesus Christ does not intend to offer a word of explanation as to that power! And that is the starting point for the belief in the infallibility of Peter and his alleged successors – when, it is fair to add, they are speaking *ex cathedra*, in virtue of their office and supposed status.

But wait a second, the same power exactly is promised to the disciples together in the context of the second occasion when Christ used the word 'church', and in the verse immediately following that reference. 'Verily I say to you, Whatsoever ye shall bind on earth shall be bound in heaven: and whatsoever ye shall loose on earth shall be loosed in heaven' (Matthew 18:18). And this time, Jesus proceeds to explain how such a thing would be possible in the case of Peter himself and in the experience of the disciples together: that which would result in their verdict on earth being one with the verdict of heaven. And the crucial thing for us to note is that Jesus Christ, in giving this answer to his disciples – and with Peter amongst them, let it be noted – was giving the answer also, to his disciples and to us, to the question that we are presently asking, namely, What is the difference between having the 'rock' in place and building the church upon that 'rock'.

But before giving the explanation Jesus Christ refers to another phenomenon which is just as remarkable as the fact that he prophesied that the decisions of his people on earth – in the complex matters of church discipline – would be one with the decisions of heaven. Here are his words: 'Again I say unto you, That if two of you shall agree on earth as touching any thing that they shall ask, it shall be done for them of my Father, which is in heaven' (Matt. 18:19). A complete equivalence between the supplications, as well as the decisions, of earth and heaven! How in (this) world could such a thing be possible? There is an explanation, says Jesus Christ. 'For where two or three are gathered together in my name, there am I in the midst of them' (Matt. 18:20). That is the explanation.

And this is also Christ's meaning when he says that he will build his church upon the rock of the experience and life of those who will come to know him. The church of Jesus Christ is not a collection of people. And certainly not a building. Rather, *it is a body of people amongst whom the Lord Jesus Christ is constantly present, leading and ruling them.* That is what he builds, once the rock is in place. He gives exactly the same truth in the upper room immediately after his resurrection: 'Then said Jesus to them again, Peace be unto you: as my Father hath sent me, even so send I you. And when he had said this, he breathed on them, and saith unto them, Receive ye the Holy Ghost: Whose soever sins ye remit, they are remitted unto them; and whose soever sins ye retain, they are retained' (John 20:21-23). Why should this be a surprise, when the Holy Spirit – the Spirit of Christ – was amongst them?

No-one has expressed it better than did Peter himself. 'To whom coming, as unto a living stone, disallowed indeed of men, but chosen of God and precious, ye also, as lively stones, are built up a spiritual house, an holy priesthood, to offer up spiritual sacrifices, acceptable to God by *Jesus Christ*' (1 Peter 2:4-5).

What should be our reaction to these things? Two things, certainly.

1. If we are truly members of the church of Jesus Christ, there should be *a sense of wonder* and of great gratitude. We belong to a great and important cause – a cause that is still advancing forwards presently – in Wales and throughout the world. The Father, no less, giving people to his Son according to the terms of the early Covenant. The Son granting

these to know him, and thereby to know the Father. (See Luke 10:22; John 17:1-3; 1 John 5:11-12; 2 Cor. 4:6.) The Son, as of old in Caesarea Philippi, confirming these and incorporating them into a body for himself, and involving himself with them, unimpeded according to the need, personally as well as corporately, himself by now having come to dwell in them – each one of them without exception!

2. *An unwavering determination to honour the Lord Jesus Christ as our only leader.* He is able to lead us. He will lead us. Chapels may close and valuable buildings fall to the ground in ruins. *'The gates of hell shall not prevail against it.'*

Believe that ye receive

From amongst the papers of J. Elwyn Davies

In the parable of the importunate widow, Jesus Christ taught his disciples to be unyielding in their importunity for seeing their petitions, which they judged to be righteous and good petitions, being answered. The best way to do this was to nurture that attitude of mind which made much of their heavenly Father. In the parable of the Pharisee and the publican he taught them to guard against the lowering of their standards and the diluting of God's demands so that they might not make light of the remnants of the sin that would remain in them. The best way for them to do that was to nurture the practice of facing up to and confessing their sinfulness and spiritual poverty, in the light of those standards.

In the upper room a little later, Jesus Christ taught his disciples how they would come to know that which he was to accomplish so that they also might accomplish it. His commands and word would be already with them; he himself, by his Spirit, would be present with them in every place and be ready to reveal to them what he would accomplish so that they might ask him for it, in his name!

A few days before he placed such emphasis on praying 'in his name', Jesus Christ gave a remarkable promise to his disciples in relation to prayer. 'And all things, whatsoever ye shall ask in prayer, believing, ye shall receive' (Matthew 21:22). 'Believe that ye receive them, and ye shall have them' (Mark 11:24). This is the account:

> Now in the morning as he returned into the city [Bethany], he hungered. And when he saw a fig tree in the way, he came to it, and found nothing thereon, but leaves only, and said unto it, 'Let no fruit grow on thee from henceforward forever.' And presently the fig tree withered away. And when the disciples saw it, they marvelled, saying, 'How soon is the fig tree withered away!' Jesus

answered and said unto them, 'Verily I say unto you, if ye have faith, and doubt not, ye shall not only do this which is done to the fig tree, but also if ye shall say unto this mountain, "Be thou removed, and be thou cast into the sea," it shall be done. *And all things, whatsoever ye shall ask in prayer, believing, ye shall receive.*

This promise is so similar in form to those other promises given by Jesus Christ in the upper room a little later (and the times when they were told to the disciples so close together) that we cannot but believe that there is good reason for this.

'And all things, whatsoever ye shall ask in prayer, believing, ye shall receive' (Matt.21:22).

'And whatsoever ye shall ask in my name, that will I do' (John 14:13).

What might the reason be? There is nothing that occurs accidentally in the life of Jesus Christ.

We can begin by saying that the disciples themselves would be certain of two things. Firstly, they would be sure that the Lord Jesus meant every word he said. He was not being capricious. Secondly, they knew that it was not very probable that Jesus Christ was suggesting that they could produce the faith he referred to by themselves.

The prayer of faith
The only way in which we can make sense of his words is by realising that Jesus Christ is here teaching his disciples one of the most basic truths regarding prayer. *If God gave the faith to believe that any one of their petitions would be granted, it would be granted.* If God gave the faith to believe it would happen, then it would happen. The lesson was that they should always be open to the possibility that God might give them the faith to believe that something particular might happen, before it happened. *This would be God's way of revealing beforehand that which he intended to accomplish.*

Jesus Christ did not offer one word in explanation of his words at the time. There is no mention either that his disciples questioned him at all. As it happened, they did not have to wait long before Jesus Christ would throw light on the matter in the upper room. They would learn from him what he intended to do as he explained to them what they were to pray for 'in his name'. They would be able to pray prayers 'in his name' because of the relationship that would exist between them, himself and the Father. With respect to those prayers, they would receive assurance in their hearts, as they prayed, that they had prayed for that which he desired.

This would not be the fruit of a self-persuasion. Nor would it be the result of a great effort on their part to assure themselves that something would certainly be granted. It would be a gift, without any tinge of uncertainty belonging to it.

God can give this conviction to his children without them having asked him for that thing 'in his name'. It is to such an event that the apostle refers in Romans 12:3, 'For I say, through the grace given unto me, to every man that is among you, not to think of himself more highly than he ought to think; but to think soberly, *according as God hath dealt to every man the measure of faith.*' And it is that faith, working quietly and consistently in the heart of those who walk with God, to which he refers in Romans 14:23: '...for whatsoever is not of faith is sin.'

What Jesus Christ explained in the upper room was the way that his disciples would discover his will *when they were ignorant of it.* When we have the faith to believe that we know what is his will, we may take steps, confident that he will enable us to fulfil that will. When we do not know his will, then, on the path of prayer, and with his Word before us, we need to seek that guidance. The comfort that he intended as he gave these promises so soon after one another and in such similar form was to enable the disciples to see how the two aspects of the Christian's experience could merge into one another.

If this is to be part of the ordinary Christian's daily experience – acting in the confidence that they are doing that which is according to the will of God – it follows that seeking to know his will should be our natural experience in our everyday lives. In that recognising the prayer that can be prayed 'in his name' is such an important part of the experience of discovering his will, it follows further that recognising that prayer, from among all the other possible petitions that we might pray, is all-important.

A Father in the Faith

But how may we recognise such prayers? The answer is simple enough. There will be three characteristics to those prayers.

Firstly, in that Jesus Christ through the Holy Spirit is the source, we would expect the prayer to reflect that truth in the spiritual integrity, depth of feeling and fervency of its expression. This is why the apostle said that the Holy Spirit would help the infirmities of the saints (when they did not know what they should pray for as they ought) *with groanings which cannot be uttered* (Rom. 8:26). Such prayers will not be superficial, but fervent prayers which we long to see answered.

Secondly, we would expect those prayers to conform completely to all his commandments and to his Word as a whole.

Thirdly, we would expect that peace, which Jesus Christ said would result from following his doctrine on prayer, to be our experience with respect to that prayer (John 14:27). It would be that same peace which the apostle Paul referred to in Philippians 4:7, 'And the peace of God, which passeth all understanding, shall keep your hearts and minds through Christ Jesus.'

Some examples
This can all happen very quickly. I remember well two occasions when I found myself facing two very difficult situations where, because I had not given the time I should have to prayer, I needed guidance very quickly. In the first case, I was on my way to meet a number of teachers from Cardiff with the purpose of seeking their agreement to form an Association of Christian Teachers in the region. I felt uncomfortable travelling on my own to a meeting which I had called, with no one there to introduce me, and certain that there would be those there who did not know me. On my way I prayed that I might know what petition I should pray in Jesus Christ's name that would correspond to that which he was intending on our behalf. For the first, and last, time in my life I found myself praying that he would make the meeting 'a happy one'. And so it was. It turned out to be one of the happiest meetings I have ever attended. A few weeks later, one of the teachers who had been present was staying with us. She said, of her own accord, 'Wasn't it a happy meeting.'

A few weeks later I was standing in the porch of a chapel in another part of Wales waiting for a monthly meeting to end so that I could hold

156

a similar meeting with the teachers of that area. I prayed again for guidance, and the result was that I found myself praying a prayer that I do not remember ever praying before or after in such a way. I cried to God that he would make me strong and firm. During the meeting I was forced to face one of the fiercest attacks against myself personally that I ever experienced. Throughout it all I was completely calm and courteous (I very much hope). I remembered the prayer given to me beforehand to pray.

On other occasions it may take a considerable time before reaching a measure of assurance what that prayer should be. But it will arrive. If we wait, prayerfully and humbly before him, it will arrive. 'Henceforth I call you not servants; for the servant knoweth not what his lord doeth,' said Jesus Christ. They shall know. What is crucial is that the disciple should acknowledge the fact that the Answerer of prayer is present with him at the time and that he is ready to enlighten him as to his will. There is nothing more sad than to think of Christians, praying on their own or with others, behaving so discourteously towards the one from whom they hope to receive answers to their prayers. The last thing they intend is to be discourteous. But is it not discourtesy in them to disregard the fact that he is present with them, in that very place, and ready to assist them to find the relevant prayers?

Further guidelines

Are there other guidelines to help us recognise the prayer that we should pray 'in the name of Jesus Christ'? Yes, there are. As the Lord Jesus promised his disciples that whatsoever they should ask 'in his name' he should do, the faithful Christian would expect a confirmation that he was on the right track *when this was true of his prayers*.

That confirmation will take two forms – negative and positive. The first form is to feel a considerable degree of frustration when praying in one direction but a measure of freedom to pray in another direction. The second form is to experience satisfaction in our souls that we are being heard in heaven as we pray. This was Christ's experience invariably as he prayed. 'Father, I thank thee that thou hast heard me. And I knew that thou hearest me always: but because of the people which stand by I said it, that they may believe that thou hast sent me' (John 11:41-42). The explanation of this is that he, in all his petitions, desired that which his Father desired and that he submitted himself completely to that which his Father wished to fulfil through him. The aim and purpose of his teaching on prayer in the upper room was to bring his disciples to that same place.

John gave a glorious description of this experience at the end of his first epistle. Firstly, he says of prayer: 'And this is the confidence that we have in him, that, if we ask anything according to his will, he heareth us.' Every Christian would agree with that statement. But the apostle then proceeds to refer to something additional that can occur when we pray: *'And if we know that he hear us, whatsoever we ask, we know that we have the petitions that we desired of him'* (1 John 5:14-15). The sense of freedom to ask changes into an assurance that we have those petitions. We would have arrived at the place Jesus Christ referred to – 'Believe that ye receive them, and ye shall have them' – that which our fathers would call 'praying through' or 'praying the prayer of faith' or 'given assurance' that the prayers had been heard. Jesus Christ used the phrase, 'Believe that ye receive'.

C. T. Studd

Some stories, especially from the missionary fields, help us to understand this. Norman Grubb in his book on C. T. Studd tells the story of when the latter and his wife, soon after they had arrived in China, determined to spend the night praying to their heavenly Father to send them money from somewhere, such was their financial crisis at the time. They got on their knees. After twenty minutes, C. T. Studd opened his eyes. There was no need for him to pray through the night in that he had received a strong sense of release and relief that his prayer had been received in heaven. And the first thing he saw was his wife, also with her eyes open for the same reason.

When the postman arrived within a fortnight, we may imagine their disappointment on finding that there was no letter in the postbag containing the expected money. C. T. Studd's conviction that his heavenly Father had heard his prayer was so strong that he turned the bag upside-down. A letter fell to the floor; it contained the note: 'I have for some reason or other received the command of God to send you a cheque for £100... God has prevented me from sleeping tonight by this command. Why He should command me to send you this I don't know – you will know better than I.' This letter changed C. T. Studd's life completely. (Norman Grubb, *C. T. Studd*, The Religious Tract Society: 1934, pp. 98-99).

J. O. Fraser

Just as wonderful is the history of J. O. Fraser soon after he had arrived in Lisuland, where he was a missionary for some years, and where he was to see a substantial harvest of converts. As a result of giving time to seek God's face in prayer, he found himself being restricted to the one petition that God would save hundreds of families. Subsequently, he also was given an assurance that God had answered his prayer. As a result he went about distributing literature over a wide region of the land in the confidence that the day would come when its contents would be appreciated. And that is what happened. As he related the story of the prayer that had been 'given' him to pray, a friend of his asked him (betraying the fact of his ignorance of these things) why he had not prayed for thousands of families! His reply? 'I could not.'

Gwilym Humphreys (1920-2010)

To come closer home, I will not soon forget Gwilym Humphreys (Harlech) turning to me after I had asked him to take family worship at our home in Eryl Aran, Bala, one Sunday night. What he had to say was unexpected, yet wonderfully encouraging. As he prayed, he said, he received assurance that God had heard our daily prayer for many months, that the Movement might own the house next door, Bryn-y-groes, for the work of the Kingdom in Wales. Although I have phrased that in the plural, and that this was true of our morning prayers, yet Gwilym was the one who was burdened. From that night onwards he continued to ask, just as he had consistently done so previously, but it was easy to see that the nature of the request was very different.

There was no indication whatever at the time that the owners were intending to move. But suddenly, one morning, as he paid the tax in the Council office, Gwilym heard that Liverpool Council was buying it as a sort of headquarters for the work of drowning Cwm Tryweryn. After fortifying us with the knowledge that our heavenly Father had heard our prayer, we went immediately to see the lady of the house. And the result – the purchase of Bryn-y-groes for the first price offered by Liverpool Council without any further bargaining, and this with great satisfaction to all concerned, including the vendor. The history of the home ever since has proved fully that God's hand was over the whole concern, including the intercession and the assurance given beforehand.

As a confirmation that this is how the promises of Jesus Christ are to be understood with respect to praying 'in his name' and obtaining assurance that they had done so, the disciples, without doubt, would have remembered the similar promise that Jesus had given them, this time with respect to praying with others, 'If two of you shall agree on earth as touching anything that they shall ask, it shall be done for them of my Father which is in heaven.'

'Believe that ye receive' would be the sign that they had prayed 'in the name of Jesus Christ' and that what they had sought would be granted, when they prayed on their own. Finding themselves in deepest agreement with others with respect to one particular petition as they prayed, would be the sign that this had happened when praying with others.

The next verse relates that they received a full explanation from Jesus Christ himself for the reason for the unanimity: 'For where two or three are gathered together in my name, there am I in the midst of them' (Matthew 18:19-20). In both cases, it is the Lord Jesus Christ, dwelling in the hearts of his saints through his Holy Spirit, who is responsible for giving to them the prayer. And its characteristic in both cases would be a deep sense of fervency and sincerity and then a peaceful satisfaction.

Christ's intention was that his disciples should think in these terms whenever they besought him to meet their need, whatever that need might be. Not that they were asking for that which seemed to them to be an obvious need but rather that they, by his great grace, were being guided to ask for that which was in agreement with his will.

It is true that we can fail. We all know how we can persuade ourselves that he has heard us – particularly when we are praying for the restoration to health of ourselves or of others and for similarly serious matters – only for this not to be true. Rather than bringing dishonour upon God's name and the Scriptures, it is better to be careful and to refrain from telling others about our expectations (other than our closest friends) until those expectations have been fulfilled. Then to bear witness for his glory.

Articles

Welcoming the doctrine

There are many good reasons for saying that the Christian should make much of the doctrine concerning prayer taught by Jesus Christ to his disciples. *Firstly, it places us in such an advantageous position, as we face our responsibilities with our Lord from day to day, if we are fortified by the assurance beforehand that our prayer has been heard.* One example of this that occurred to a group of us in the early days of running Evangelical Movement camps stands out in the memory. It is worth recording here.

Glynllifon Camp

I had promised to go on the Friday night to give the last evangelistic message of the Camp held that year at Glynllifon, near Caernarfon. At mid-day I received a phone-call. There was no need for to me to go there to evangelise. A number had been converted at the morning meeting. I was welcome to come, but would I bring a message relevant for new-born believers! I was given some idea over the phone that something significant had happened during the morning service.

I was given a message as I finished my afternoon's work, and I was also given unusual freedom to speak. To my great surprise, the leader of the meeting gave an opportunity to any who wished to pray publicly. For the first time in my life I heard young people thanking God warmly for sending the Holy Spirit to the morning service! Later that night, I was given the whole story from the man who had preached the messages in the morning meetings of the week – the Rev. Arthur Pritchard.

It was not something new for me to hear him say that he had not slept much all week, worrying each night over his message for the morning. (He was a bad sleeper away from home, at the best of times.) The previous night (Thursday night) he had happened to pass one of the officers' rooms and heard some of them praying. He opened the door slightly and listened to them. He soon realised that there was something different in the prayers. He joined the company. They prayed one after the other for some time. Then, he said, each one of them received an assurance that God had heard their prayer that he would send the Holy Spirit to the morning meeting. The conviction was so strong, he slept soundly all night. Before he gave his morning address, he agreed with the officer leading it that an appropriate hymn to sing after the message would be one of Nantlais's hymns, '*Fe ddaeth yr Ysbryd Glân, mae'n gweithio yma'n awr.'[75]* And that is what happened. Some of the sheaves that were gathered into the Kingdom that morning are with us still, bearing their witness to his love and grace.

A second reason why we should make much of the teaching that Jesus Christ gave on prayer is this. *God sees fit to prepare his people for that which he intends to do by leading them to pray for it beforehand.*

The Annual Conferences

One of the most sacred features of the annual Conferences of the Evangelical Movement of Wales, both the Welsh and English conferences, which I had the privilege to attend for many years, was experiencing time and again a knowledge given to us unfailingly as to the nature of the 11 o'clock morning service by the measure of freedom felt in the 9.30 prayer meeting. I remember one Conference when the speaker was preaching in a masterly fashion, yet not touching the hearts of his hearers at all. Remarkable freedom was given to pray for the following service one morning. The preacher's admission afterwards was that he had no idea what had happened to him in the pulpit, such was the anointing upon him and the blessing that followed.

Evangelising services

I remember another occasion when four or five of us used to go to Cardiganshire to take two evangelistic services between us in various localities, staying for the two days at the home of the Rev. and Mrs Vernon Higham in Llanddewibrefi. While the Rev. Gwilym Humphreys and I were away from home, our wives and two others, who were staying at Eryl Aran, Bala, at the time held a prayer meeting, praying for us during the times of the services. That particular night, we felt completely shackled as we sought to minister, so much so that we came to the conclusion that we could never show our faces in that chapel again – let alone preach there the following day according to our engagement. The other brethren would have to fill in for us. Our intention was to depart for home immediately. We decided to phone home in order to prepare them for our arrival. After reciting our story and sharing our decision, there came a voice from the other end responding quietly and without fuss, 'How strange,' it said, 'we had no freedom at all to pray for you tonight but remarkable freedom in praying for you tomorrow night.' We had to stay. Their expectations on the morrow were fully realised.

Another reason for making much of Christ's teaching on prayer is the following. *By 'giving' prayer, before an event, or independently of an event, God ensures his glory.* When the prayer is made known, after the event, it is evident to all that all was from Him. It is God's way of adding his signature to his workmanship.

D. Eryl Davies

I venture to add one more sacred memory of another occasion. An important post in a Christian institution was being offered to an individual (the Rev. Dr D. Eryl Davies). He was ready to accept but was unable to do so because of objections that a colleague would raise. I was asked to be present while the two met to see if they could come to some understanding with respect to these objections. Things seemed very dark for us for some time. Then, suddenly, the two of us realised that an amazing change had come about in the attitude of the one making the objections. We were now discussing matters with a completely different person to the one with whom we had begun our conversation. In the light of what happened, the post was accepted.

That night the person appointed had a phone-call from a friend who was anxious to know what had been happening to him at a particular time that morning. 'I was forced,' he said, 'to go apart and pray for you until I had an assurance that my prayer had been heard, and that a blessing would follow.' It was at that exact time that the transformation had occurred which we could not for the life of us account for.

A Christian is to walk with God 'in the light' at all times. 'If we walk in the light... we have fellowship one with another (that is, with the Father and the Son), and the blood of Jesus Christ his Son cleanseth us from all sin', says John (1 John 1:7). This means that we are constantly seeking to know God's will and what Jesus Christ intends to accomplish in us and through us. When we remember all the situations and all the needs that surround us on all sides, the believer also wishes to know for whom and what he should intercede and what action he then should take if called upon to do so.

In every case, the answer is the same: the prayer must be sought. And it must be remembered that the way to recognise it is by the weight of the longing within us and the liberty given to pray it. The way in which we are satisfied that our petition will be granted is by being assured without question that we shall receive what we asked for.

Notes

1   'The Gold Gate – Remembering J. Elwyn Davies.'

2   Mair Eluned Davies, 'Dyddiadau Elwyn a rhai o'i nodweddion' [Elwyn's dates and some of his characteristics], (Unpublished article, March 2007), 4.

3   Noel Gibbard, *Taught to Serve: The History of Barry and Bryntirion Colleges* (Bridgend: Evangelical Press of Wales, 1996).

4   Mair Eluned Davies, 'Dyddiadau Elwyn a rhai o'i nodweddion' [Elwyn's dates and some of his characteristics], (Unpublished article, March 2007).

5   J. Elwyn Davies, *O! Ryfedd Ras* ['O! Wondrous Grace'], (Bridgend: Bryntirion Press, 1998), 19.

6   Davies, *O! Ryfedd Ras*, 23.

7   Davies, *O! Ryfedd Ras*, 24.

8   Davies, *O! Ryfedd Ras*, 18.

9   Davies, *O! Ryfedd Ras* 19-20.

10   Davies, *O! Ryfedd Ras*, 61-62.

11   Davies, *O! Ryfedd Ras*, 105.

12   Davies, *O! Ryfedd Ras* 47.

13   Davies, *O! Ryfedd Ras*, 48.

14   D. Densil Morgan, *The Span of the Cross: Christian Religion and Society in Wales 1914-2000* (Cardiff: University of Wales Press, 1999), 248.

15   Interview with the Rev. J. Elwyn Davies reported by John Emyr, 21 November 1992 (Unpublished).

16   Emyr Roberts, *Cyrraedd Trwy'r Glustog* (Denbigh: Gwasg Gee, 1971), 17.

17   Roberts, *Cyrraedd Trwy'r Glustog*, 24

18 Robert Pope, *Codi Muriau Dinas Duw: Anghydffurfiaeth ac Anghydffurfwyr Cymru'r Ugeinfed Ganrif* [Raising the Walls of the City of God: The Nonconformity and Nonconformists of Twentieth Century Wales] (Bangor: Centre for the Advanced Study of Religion in Wales, University of Wales, Bangor, 2005), 187.

19 Pope, *Codi Muriau Duw*, 45.

20 Interview, 9.

21 Interview, 11.

22 Interview, 12.

23 The words of Bobi Jones and R. Geraint Gruffydd are quoted in Emyr Roberts, *Cyrraedd Trwy'r Glustog*, 62.

24 'The Biblical Doctrine of Error': author's notes.

25 J. Elwyn Davies, 'God's Gift to a Nation', *The Evangelical Magazine of Wales,* April 1981, 26. See below, 139.

26 Alister E. McGrath, *Christian Spirituality*, (Oxford: Blackwell Publishers, 1999), 27-28.

27 R. Geraint Gruffydd, *Y Ffordd Gadarn: Ysgrifau ar Lên a Chrefydd* [The Firm Highway: Essays on Literature and Religion] ed. by E. Wyn James, (Bridgend: Bryntirion Press, 2008), 340. See below, 45.

28 J. Elwyn Davies, 'Addoli mewn Ysbryd a Gwirionedd' ['Worshipping in Spirit and in Truth']: From *Anerchiadau Cynhadledd Gweinidogion* ['Ministers' Conference Addresses'], 1991, 5.

29 J. Elwyn Davies, ' "Yr Hyn a Wyddom" – Epistemeg Gristnogol ["What we Know" – Christian Epistemology]' *Ysgrifau Diwinyddol [Theological Essays]*, I, Golygydd Noel A. Gibbard (Evangelical Press of Wales, 1979), 50-51.

30 Idris Charles, *Heb y Mwgwd* [Without the Mask] (Tal-y-bont, 2008), 107.

31 Worldwide Evangelisation Crusade – a well-known evangelical missionary society.

32 Mair Eluned Davies, 'Elwyn's dates and some of his characteristics'.

33 p. 68.

34 Personal notes.

35 *The Evangelical Magazine.* This is the sister magazine to the English periodical of the same name. It was first published in 1948, seven years before its English counterpart.

36 J. Elwyn Davies, *Gwrthgilwyr Diarwybod* ['Unconscious Backsliders'], *Y Cylchgrawn Efengylaidd*, Volume 3, Number V, (Spring/Summer 1956), 22. See below, 134.

Notes

37   See below, 135.

38   A work in progress by the author dealing with the history, theology and influence of the Bala Evangelical Ministers' Conference (1955-2012) to be published in 2013.

39   Noel Gibbard, *The First Fifty Years: The History of the Evangelical Movement of Wales 1948-1998* (Bridgend: Bryntirion Press, 2002), 23.

40   J. Elwyn Davies, *Striving Together: The Evangelical Movement of Wales – its principles and aims* (Bridgend: Evangelical Press of Wales, 1984), 14.

41   Davies, *Striving Together*, 12.

42   Interview, 3.

43   Davies, *Striving Together*, 12.

44   Meetings in which believers share their spiritual experiences.

45   D. Martyn Lloyd-Jones, *Llais y Doctor: Detholiad o waith Cyhoeddedig Cymraeg Dr Martyn Lloyd-Jones* [The Doctor's Voice: An Anthology of the Published works in Welsh of Dr Martyn Lloyd-Jones] (Bridgend: Bryntirion Press, 1999), 90.

46   J. Elwyn Davies, *The United Church of Wales: Comments on the report of the Joint Committee of the Four Denominations* (Port Talbot: Evangelical Movement of Wales), n.d.

47   Morgan, *The Span of the Cross*, 217.

48   Morgan, *The Span of the Cross*, 248.

49   Entitled 'Cytûn' from 1999 onwards.

50   Noel A. Davies, *A History of Ecumenism in Wales 1956-1990* (Cardiff: University of Wales Press, 2008), 31.

51   Written in its final form by Graham Harrison and published by the Evangelical Movement of Wales Press in 1966. A Welsh version, *Yr Eglwys Gristnogol*, written in its final form by the Rev. Emyr Roberts, another Bala Conference member, was published in 1966.

52   Noel Gibbard, *The First Fifty Years*, 156.

53   Davies, *Striving Together*, 17.

54   Davies, *Striving Together*, 33.

55   Davies, *Striving Together*, 8-9.

56   Now entitled Affinity.

57   Davies, *Striving Together*, 35.

58   Gibbard, *The First Fifty Years*, 21.

59 Davies, ' "Yr Hyn a Wyddom" – Epistemeg Gristnogol', [' "What we Know" – Christian Epistemology'], *Ysgrifau Diwinyddol* [Theological Essays], 1, 52.

60 Lloyd-Jones, *Llais y Doctor,* 95.

61 Gibbard, *The First Fifty Years,* 25.

62 Gibbard, *The First Fifty Years,* 22.

63 'O! Wondrous Grace.'

64 Castle Square, Caernarfon.

65 The local Urdd (the Welsh League of Youth) centre.

66 Brynuchaf, Llanymawddwy – the farmhouse which was the home of John and Mari Jones. Mari Jones is the author of the well-known books: *In the Shadow of Aran, In the Shelter of the Fold,* and *When Swallows Return.*

67 The sisters Emily and Wena Roberts. Their home in Llanymawddwy was an open home to Christians from all over Wales at this time. Emily in particular was the main distributor of the magazine, *Y Cylchgrawn Efengylaidd,* throughout Wales.

68 By William Williams, Pantycelyn.

69 By William Williams, Pantycelyn.

70 A centre for Welsh activities in Cardiff.

71 'The Evangelist', a periodical published in the period 1909-39.

72 From the hymn, 'O llefara, addfwyn Iesu' ('Speak, I pray Thee, gentle Jesus!') by Williams, Pantycelyn.

73 'glorious host': taken from the poem 'Cymru' by D. Gwenallt Jones, (*Ysgubau'r Awen,* 1938).

74 A Welsh weekly newspaper.

75 'The Holy Spirit has come, He's working here now.'